The Last Days with the Two Witnesses

TINA M. MOORE

Fulton Books, Inc.
Meadville, PA

Published by Fulton Books 2023

ISBN 979-8-88731-351-1 (paperback)
ISBN 979-8-88731-352-8 (digital)

Printed in the United States of America

This one is for my parents, who piqued my interest about the two witnesses of Revelation 11, even as a small child. The dinner table discussions we held concerning the end times were the seeds planted for this writing.

Contents

Introduction..vii

The Role of the Two Witnesses in an Ancient Jewish Wedding........1

The Two Prophets Who Tormented the Earth.............................6

The Fire of the Two Witnesses..14

When the Counterfeit Hits a Wall...20

The Beast from the Bottomless Pit..28

The Two Who Bring Oil...39

The Golden Oil...47

The Outer Court of the Temple...53

The Two Olive Trees...63

Cutting Off the Horseleech..78

The Staggering Effects of Strong Delusion.................................86

The Elijah Mantle on the Two Witnesses...................................100

The Gnashing of Teeth..113

Trampling the Serpent's Seed...127

The Fruit That Remains...138

Introduction

In his letter to the Ephesians, Paul compares the union of husband and wife to that of Christ and the Church. The two witnesses of Revelation 11 are the most important figures involved in the impending (metaphorical) wedding that is to come between the Groom and His bride.

These two end-time prophets will ultimately lay their lives down for the Church so that she is prepared for the Groom when He arrives. They are selfless, humble, yet bold and powerful. When the time arrives for them to step on the global scene to battle the harlot Babylonian system and her leader, the Antichrist, God's two consecrated representatives will already understand their purpose in purifying the global Church. Before they ever begin to operate in the anointing that will be granted to them in their offices (as prophets), they will have found themselves in the Bible and acknowledged their roles as witnesses in the wedding. They will lay down their lives as martyrs, leaving behind them an illuminated pathway for the corporate body of Christ to follow. Believers and unbelievers alike will know them, considering that their faces, voices, and reputations will be widely publicized to every nation and tongues of people. Their lives and ministries will be followed by the largest worldwide television networks because God is going to ensure that their message is heard far and wide before they are taken up into glory. They will publish the gospel of Jesus Christ across the land and prophesy according to the Word of the Lord. God has foreordained them to approve of His Son's wedding. His reason for sending the witnesses is to help the Church (the bride) prepare to meet the Bridegroom in the air. The Church, however, will not be properly adorned for the wedding until the spirit of reconciliation that accompanies the ministries of

God's two end-time prophets unifies the corporate body. Upon their ascension into glory, they will pass down the Elijah mantle to God's pastors, leaders, and all who are willing to make the journey for the golden oil. As a result, many *Elishas* will pick up the mantle and distribute the golden oil to those who are staggering under the intoxicating effects of Babylon's cup of strong delusion. The brilliant light that shines upon the Church will set her ablaze, creating a chasm between the righteous and the counterfeit impostors who work iniquity. In turn, the Church will remove herself from the stumbling blocks, and those who work evil will be locked outside the city—the city of the great king!

The Role of the Two Witnesses in an Ancient Jewish Wedding

The ancient Jewish wedding has special relevance to the time in which we live because these are the days that immediately precede the return of the Messiah for His bride. When Jesus returns in the clouds to carry us away with Him, He will not return as a teacher, a carpenter, a rabbi, or a shepherd. No. At that time, He will come as a bridegroom, which was taught in Jesus's parable of the ten virgins. In order for the Church to receive an open revelation of Christ as *the Bridegroom*, she must understand the ancient Jewish wedding customs that Jesus practiced in taking a bride for himself.

The entire Bible is about a marriage covenant, both old and new. It chronicles the love relationship between God and His people. Although many believers have a legalistic view of the Bible as a rule book, it is actually a love letter written from the Father of the Bridegroom for His Son's bride, spelling out all the blessings given to her.

Although God kept His part of the covenant with Israel, Israel's heart was turned toward their idols to worship foreign gods (Jer. 31:32). As a result, God proposed a love covenant with non-Jews (Gentiles).

Before the Bridegroom can return, however, His bride must be properly adorned for the wedding. The scriptures have a lot to say about wedding garments. Isaiah 61:10 says, "I delight greatly in the Lord; my soul rejoices in my God. For he has clothed me with garments of salvation and arrayed me in a robe of his righteousness, as a bridegroom adorns his head like a priest, and as a bride adorns herself with her jewels."

The Church should be adorning herself in preparation for the impending wedding with Christ as she washes her white robes with the blood of Jesus. Through the sanctifying work of the Holy Spirit, the bride will one day stand before the Bridegroom without a spot or wrinkle:

> So that he may present the church to himself as glorious—not having a stain or wrinkle, or any such blemish, but holy and blameless. (Eph. 5:27)

In a parable, Jesus taught about a man who was not properly dressed for His Son's wedding banquet. As a result, the man was cast into the outer darkness.

The wedding day is fast approaching, and those who have not washed their garments in the blood of Jesus will not be properly dressed for the wedding. They, too, will be cast out and excluded as part of the conglomeration of the saints who make up the bride of Christ. Revelation 22:14 says, "Blessed are those who wash their robes. They will be permitted to enter through the gates of the city and eat the fruit from the tree of life."

The Bridegroom is not returning for a defiled people but for a virgin bride whose garments are as white as snow (Isa. 1:18).

We have all been called to be a part of the Messiah's bride. In ancient Jewish history, the bride was often chosen by the father of the bridegroom. An example of this in the Bible can be found in the book of Genesis when Abraham sent his servant Eliezer to find a bride for his son Isaac. In the same fashion, God has chosen the Church to be the virgin bride that His Son will return for. Jesus revealed this in John 15:16:

> You did not choose me, but I chose you and appointed you so that you might go and bear fruit—fruit that will last...

Scriptures say we love Him because He first loved us (1 John 4:19). The Father has chosen us!

In those times, brides were bought at a price. This is evident when Jacob worked for his bride's father, Laban, to purchase Rachel. Genesis 29:20 says, "So Jacob worked seven years to pay for Rachel."

Since wives were purchased, they belonged to their husbands. Although this practice seems unjust, it actually raised the bar on marriage. On the other hand, when a pagan wished to marry, he would take a woman to his house and have sexual intercourse with her without having to purchase her and without the consent and support of the two witnesses. There was no value placed on the bride in the pagan world. According to Jewish custom, when the groom purchased his wife, it proved that women were to be both sought after and cherished. Men were to work to acquire her because she had value! First Corinthians 6:20 says, "You were bought with a price [you were actually purchased with the precious blood of Jesus and made His own]. So then, honor and glorify God with your body."

Knowing that we were bought at such a high price, the blood of Jesus gives us confidence in the love the Father has toward us.

Our value can be likened to the parable about the merchant who found a pearl of great price. The pearl carried so much value that he was willing to sell everything he owned to buy it. That is what the Father did for us. He saw so much value in His created man that He gave up what was most dear to Himself (the precious blood of His only Son) in order to buy us back.

When Christ was hanging on the cross, His last words before His death were these: "It is finished" (John 19:30). And with that, He bowed His head and gave up His Spirit.

The word *finished* here is *teleó*, which means "to bring to an end, complete, fulfill, to pay in full." Therefore, "It is finished!" had bridal overtones. As Jesus hung on the cross, the last thing on His mind was His bride and the price He was paying for her! Another word used to describe the *finishing* work of Christ on the cross is *consummation*. *Consummation* means "to make (a marriage or relationship) complete by having sexual intercourse." In ancient history, a Jewish wedding was complete when sexual intercourse between the couple occurred.

God uses the greatest example of intimacy on earth, the marriage covenant between a bridegroom and his bride, to reveal the intimacy that a believer can have with God. First Corinthians 6:17 says, "But whoever is united with the Lord is one with him in spirit."

Paul writes to the Corinthian Church about the relationship between Christ and His bride:

> I am jealous for you with a godly jealousy. I promised you to one husband, to Christ, so that I might present you as a pure virgin to him. (2 Cor. 11:2)

In Jewish society, the parents of the betrothed generally drew up the marriage contract. Symbolically, God has done the same; He has drawn up His covenant with the bride of Christ (often referred to as *the Church)* and has revealed His Son to her in every way possible (through the medium of His Word).

Traditionally, the bride and groom would meet, perhaps for the first time, when the marriage contract was signed. Although the couple was *considered* married at this point, they would separate until the actual time of the wedding ceremony. They would each go their own way: the bride would usually remain in her parents' home, and the groom would leave to prepare their new home, which could require a considerable amount of time. When the home was established and everything was in place, the groom would return for his bride without notice. The marriage ceremony would then take place, and the wedding banquet would follow.

Although the wedding ceremony has not yet commenced between the bride of Christ and her Groom, the contract has been made (through the medium of the Word) and the covenant sealed (with the blood of the Groom), the spotless Lamb of God who laid His life down for His soon-to-be bride. In a sense, the bride has already met the Groom through her intimate connection with His Word, as she also hides Him in her heart, yet she awaits His soon return to consummate the wedding ceremony.

With that said, the two witnesses were possibly the most important figures at the wedding because they were the entities who legitimized the marriage. As a matter of fact, the marriage covenant in those days was not binding without their consent. It had to be signed and approved by the *two appointed ones*, who were specifically chosen by the father of the bridegroom (which was the primary duty of the best man and the bridesmaid). Their signatures not only made the union legal (sealed the marriage) but were also required before the wedding ceremony could occur. It was also proof that they supported the couple.

Even before the wedding ceremony ever took place, the groom would agree to be bound by the terms of the marriage contract in the presence of two witnesses.

Could this mean that the two witnesses will be present for the marriage contract? I believe it does. No one can really be certain about the order of events involving Christ's return unless God has personally revealed it to them Himself. Perhaps the two prophets are here for the initial marriage contract but are martyred before the return of Christ (the wedding).

What *is* certain is that God's two appointed ones will be vital for purifying the Church, adorning her with the proper wedding attire, and helping her to buy the oil necessary to complete her journey.

Undoubtedly, then, it was a prestigious honor to be selected as a witness. It meant that you were highly trusted and loved by the bride and the groom. The witnesses were deeply connected with the married couple because their blessing was upon it.

In the same fashion, God has appointed two end-time prophets as witnesses who approve the marriage of the Lamb to His glorious bride. God has selected the Church as His Son's bride, and the two witnesses will not approve of the wedding until the bride of Christ has removed herself from Babylon and washed her garments in the blood of the Lamb, and only then will she be worthy of entering the bridal chamber.

The Two Prophets Who Tormented the Earth

Revelation 11 indicates that after the completion of their testimonies, the beast that ascends from the bottomless pit will overcome the two witnesses by killing them and leaving their dead bodies in the street for the curious gaze of spectators. Therefore, they are predestined to die as martyrs according to the Word of God. Undoubtedly, the two prophets who are chosen for this end-time ministry will surrender to martyrdom well in advance, prior to accepting the call of God and before ever walking in this office. As a matter of fact, the word *witness* here in Revelation 11:3 is *martus*, where we get our word *martyr*, "one who willingly lays down his life for his religious beliefs." According to the *Strong's Concordance*, the two witnesses will be murdered because they are relentless in faithfully interpreting God's counsels.

Because they have the power to shut heaven (so that no rain falls in the days of their prophecy) and because they have power over waters (to turn them to blood) and seeing that they will strike the earth with all forms of plagues (as often as they desire), scriptures indicate that the people of the earth will literally rejoice over the deaths of the two witnesses because they "tormented" those who dwell upon the earth.

> And those who dwell on the earth will rejoice over them, make merry, and send gifts to one another, because these two prophets tormented those who dwell on the earth. (Rev. 11:10)

However, this type of mistreatment puts the two prophets in good company with the surrounding cloud of witnesses who paved the path before them. These were the spiritual forerunners who endured the same persecution, even in the Old Testament (Heb. 12:1). God's greatest prophets have always been accused of being dissenters, troublemakers, and the like.

Let's look at the prophet Moses, for example. The Pharaoh's servants perceived that keeping Moses around was becoming problematic to the entire kingdom of Egypt. They asked the Pharaoh,

> How long shall this man be a snare to us? Let the
> men go, that they may serve the LORD their God.
> Do you not yet know that Egypt is destroyed?
> (Exod. 10:7)

The prophet Moses was accused of destroying the Egyptian land and kingdom. He was considered a "snare" to the Pharaoh, his magicians, and to the kingdom of witchcraft. The word *snare* in this verse is *moqesh*, defined as "bait or lure, a snare, figurative of what allures and entraps any one to disaster or ruin." Furthermore, the word *moqesh* comes from *yaqosh*, which is "a noose [for catching animals], a hook [for the nose], trap, be ensnared" (*Strong's Concordance*).

The Pharaoh's grip on God's people proved to be disastrous for the entire land of Egypt as the prophet Moses was inspired by God to pronounce grievous curses upon land, cattle, and people. Every wicked plot of the Pharaoh to cage the Hebrew people backfired on him. The Egyptians began to believe that Moses was the snare, the bringer of bad luck who led them to their complete and utter destruction.

However, Moses was merely seeking God's will, which included deliverance from wicked Egyptian bondage on behalf of his people. The stout-hearted Pharaoh was resistant to the word of God to let God's people go, for such is the nature of the enemy. He doesn't seem to let go easily.

God spoke through the prophet Isaiah concerning Satan's stubborn resistance to letting God's people free:

> Who [Satan] made the world as a wilderness And
> destroyed its cities, Who did not open the house
> of his prisoners? (Isa. 14:17)

This verse speaks of satanic imprisonment. As a fowler ensnares a bird to his cage, Satan lays bait and draws man in; with his hook in their nose, he pulls them closer until he can lock the door to their confinement. He uses his human instruments for this craft. These are workers of iniquity, influenced by evil spirits concerning the art of manipulation, intimidation, and domination. This practice is called witchcraft, and it is a counterfeit for the freedom that is found in the authentic power of God's love. The power of witchcraft draws man away from the truth by luring him into the cages of sin. Notice this verse found in Jeremiah:

> For among My people are found wicked men;
> They lie in wait as one who sets snares; They set
> a trap; They catch men. As a cage is full of birds,
> So their houses are full of deceit. Therefore they
> have become great and grown rich. (Jer. 5:26–27)

Again, these are men catching men. However, as God begins to raise up prophets like Moses and the two witnesses of Revelation 11 who deliver the authoritative prophecies of God, saying, "Let my people out of this cage!" the kingdom of witchcraft will begin to shout accusations at God's anointed ones. When the enemy starts losing his hold on the subjects he has bound, he will begin to hurl insults! In the case of Moses versus Pharaoh, the kingdom of witchcraft was losing the battle to the Most High God, and the Egyptians were convinced that it was the prophet of God who was a snare for *them*! Moses was delivering harsh blows to the prison bars of satanic resistance that held the Hebrews in bondage to slavery, but now he is the man viewed as a "snare" to their occult system!

Moses wasn't the only prophet in the Bible accused of bringing turmoil to the kingdom of witchcraft. Paul the Apostle stood trial before the Roman governor for being a "troublemaker." His opposers falsely accused him of being a snare to them:

> We have found this man [Paul] to be a nuisance, stirring up dissension among the Jews all over the world. He is a ringleader of the sect of the Nazarenes, and he even tried to desecrate the temple; so we seized him. (Acts 24:5–6)

However, Paul denied the claims made against him in court by stating that he wasn't at all creating dissension among the people but merely worshipping the God of their ancestors. His rebuttal is found in Acts 24:

> My accusers did not find me arguing with anyone at the temple, or stirring up a crowd in the synagogues or anywhere else in the city. And they cannot prove to you the charges they are now making against me. However, I admit that I worship the God of our ancestors as a follower of the Way, which they call a sect. (Acts 24:12–14)

Paul was also blamed for causing riots in Antioch, Thessalonica, Berea, Corinth, Ephesus, and Jerusalem. On one of their missions, the entire city rose up together against Paul and Silas after they had cast the spirit of divination from the slave girl. The magistrates were so irate that they tore off their clothes and commanded the two be beaten with rods. The words of their accusers are found in Acts 16:20:

"These men, being Jews, exceedingly trouble our city…"

Consider also Elijah the prophet who was perceived by Ahab to be a snare to his false religious kingdom of Israel:

> When he [Ahab] saw Elijah, he said to him, "Is that you, you troubler of Israel?" "I have not made trouble for Israel," Elijah replied. "But you and your father's family have. You have aban-

doned the Lord's commands and have followed
the Baals." (1 Kings 18:16–18)

At this juncture, it had not rained in Israel for over three years according to Elijah's prophecy, hence the reason for the slanderous comment of Ahab toward Elijah here in this passage. Elijah had commanded the skies to be shut so that the land would receive no rain:

> I serve the LORD, the God of Israel, Elijah said
> to Ahab. "As surely as the LORD lives, no rain or
> dew will fall during the next few years unless I
> command it." (1 Kings 17:1)

As a result of Elijah's declaration, there was a severe famine in the land. For this reason, Ahab accused the prophet of "troubling" Israel. Elijah was viewed as a "troubler" in Israel for the same reasons that Moses was perceived as a "snare" in the eyes of all in Egypt. And for the same reasons, Paul and Silas were viewed as "troublemakers" in the cities where they preached the gospel.

The kingdom of Babylon weeps over her losses to God's righteous people who implement His government on earth. Satan begins to "blow out" when the bands of wickedness begin to loosen, the burdens unravel, the oppressed are made free, and the yokes are destroyed off humanity. Satan will begin to accuse God (and His prophets) of unjust acts of violence. But God is a god of vengeance, and He will resort to drastic measures to ensure that His people are released from Egyptian bondage into their newfound freedoms. Moses instructed the Pharaoh to let His people go!

In the book of Ezekiel, God sent a strong warning against false prophets who were entangling His people in their web of witchcraft:

> Therefore thus says the Lord GOD: "Behold, I am
> against your magic charms by which you hunt
> souls there like birds. I will tear them from your
> arms, and let the souls go, the souls you hunt like
> birds. I will also tear off your veils and deliver My

people out of your hand, and they shall no longer be as prey in your hand. Then you shall know that I am the LORD." (Ezek. 13:20–21)

Satan is a hunter. He opposes freedom by encapsulating the souls of men. He uses his human instruments (workers of iniquity) who plan this imprisonment. God speaks concerning the meditations of their hearts:

Woe to those who devise wickedness and work evil on their beds! When the morning dawns, they perform it, because it is in the power of their hands. They covet fields and seize them, and houses, and take them away; they oppress a man and his house, a man and his inheritance. (Mic. 2:1–2)

Because of this orchestrated confinement, God has ordered "binding and loosing" as a form of effective prayer against these foes of His grace. As men of God begin to walk in the office of the prophet, God takes control over the demonic forces that bind His people. He will "loosen" the bands of wickedness when His oracles open their mouths to say, "Thus says the Lord." As men begin to exercise their authority through prophecy, the enemy will be required to *let God's people go.*

On the other hand, as God begins to liberate the souls who are bound, spiritual darkness will sense that they are losing ground. They'll believe they're the kingdom being confined, this time by *God's chains.* An example of this can be found in Psalm 2:

Why are the nations in tumultuous agitation, and why do the peoples meditate a vain thing? The kings of the earth take their stand and the rulers gather together, against the LORD and against His Anointed One, saying, "Let us break Their chains and cast away Their cords." The

> One enthroned in heaven laughs; the Lord taunts
> them… (Ps. 2:1–4)

You see, as anointed men begin to command, "Let God's people go!" the forces of darkness will begin to feel the effects of being bound (caged) by *God's* chains (cords). The prayer of binding and loosing is mentioned in the New Testament. Jesus said,

> Assuredly, I say to you, whatever you bind on earth will be bound in heaven, and whatever you loose on earth will be loosed in heaven. Again I say to you that if two of you agree on earth concerning anything that they ask, it will be done for them by My Father in heaven. (Matt. 18:18–19)

Two or three believers bound together in an agreement can bind, release, and alter the order of things on the earth. In Jesus's parable of the wedding banquet, a man who wasn't wearing wedding clothes was bound by his hands and feet and cast into outer darkness, a place of weeping and gnashing of teeth.

> Then the king said to the servants, "Bind him hand and foot, and throw him into the outer darkness; in that place there will be weeping and gnashing of teeth." (Matt. 22:13)

In another of Jesus's parables of the wheat and the weeds, Jesus commanded that the weeds be "bound" or "tied into bundles" to be thrown into the fire for separation:

> Let both grow together until the harvest, and at harvest time I will tell the reapers, "Gather the weeds first and bind them in bundles to be burned, but gather the wheat into my barn." (Matt. 13:30)

Notice in this passage how the good wheat will also be bound together in the end. It is God (and His servants) who should be binding, loosing, restraining, and casting out.

As God's people begin to bind (cage) the powers of witchcraft in these last days, they will be faced with the same resistance and accusations as the patriarchs of old. If the enemy is not hurling insults our way or calling us a "snare," "troubler," "dissenter," or a "nuisance," then we are not currently winning against the kingdom of Babylon. We must walk in the authority of the Bible "greats" aforementioned, as they are ensamples for us who are escaping our own type of Egyptian slavery in pursuit of our modern-day promised land.

We will begin to see these sorts of things happen again very soon. The two witnesses will be the modern-day Moses, Elijah, and Paul who "trouble," "torment," and "irritate" the darkness. The body of Christ should remember these things and lift them up in prayer as opposed to joining the world in hurling insults at them. The Church should be careful to avoid being a part of accusing these two anointed ones because the judgments they will soon release upon the kingdom of Babylon will fall upon the members who comprise it. The two witnesses will battle the Antichrist in a series of showdowns, much like Moses and the Pharaoh's magicians who tried to replicate the plagues. The stories that we have read in the Bible, Moses versus Pharaoh and Elijah versus Ahab and Jezebel, will become realities again when the Antichrist steps on the scene to take rule over the world. The two witnesses will openly battle the beast just as in the days of old. The Church should prepare herself to surround these two prophets who stand boldly to deliver the "now word" for the hour in which we live.

The book of Revelation proves that Babylon must fall (Rev. 17–18). Accordingly, when these things appear and she begins to suffer from the plagues rendered to her, let us rejoice that the mantle of Elijah and Moses have fallen upon the two end-time prophets of Revelation 11.

The Fire of the Two Witnesses

In Revelation 11, the scriptures reveal how the two appointed witnesses whose prophecies are reserved for the end of times will literally have the power of God emanating from their mouths with such force that anyone who stands up to oppose His work through them will be devoured.

> And if anyone wants to harm them, fire proceeds
> from their mouths and devours their enemies.
> And if anyone wants to harm them, he must be
> killed in this manner. (Rev. 11:5)

The verse aforementioned says that punishment would be issued to those who attempt to harm the two prophets. The word *harm* is *adikeó*, which means "to do wrong, to act wickedly, to act contrary to what is *divinely approved*, especially to inflict undeserved hurt by *ignoring God's justice*."

In other words, there will be people who believe that the prophets are acting out of the wrong kind of spirit. They will ask, "Who, after all, would call down plagues upon the earth that prove catastrophic to so many lives?" In reality, the acts of the two witnesses will be God's judgment upon those who have not received the mark of God, which parallels the Old Testament account when God's people applied the blood of Jesus to their doorposts for protection. Refuters will be "harming" these prophets by acting contrary to what God has already (divinely) approved through them, seeing that He has authorized these things. It will be God's final act of justice for those whose hearts have chosen Him.

People of all nations will oppose the ministries, testimonies, and judgments that the prophets render upon those who stand as stumbling blocks to God's building endeavors. Revelation 11:5 says that anyone who wants to harm them (by being contrary to their ministries in any way) must be killed. This means just what it says: "put to death, killed and abolished" (*Strong's Concordance*).

Although it may be difficult to imagine such grim consequences for those who are objectionable to God's building endeavors, this type of judgment has been rendered by God's prophets throughout the course of Bible history. In addition, God has always used fire as the element to destroy Satan's idols. Through the prophet Jeremiah, God revealed that He would make His words a fire that would emanate from the mouth when spoken. Fire from a prophet's mouth was symbolic of the consuming effect it would have on the listeners if they chose to cling to their idols instead of the words of their Creator. God said to Jeremiah,

> Because you have spoken this word, I will make
> My words a fire in your mouth and this people
> the wood it consumes. (Jer. 5:14)

In other words, God's words (when spoken) are so anointed that those who reject the message would not only be burned but also consumed. This was demonstrated through Elijah and Moses, two prophets in the Old Testament. One day, the pagan king Ahaziah sent to Elijah a captain of fifty men with this message:

> Man of God, the king has said, "Come down!"
> Elijah answered the captain, "If I am a man of
> God, may fire come down from heaven and con-
> sume you and your fifty men." And fire came
> down from heaven and consumed the captain
> and his fifty men. (2 Kings 1:10)

Notice that God used *fire* to distinguish between the false and the authentic. Witchcraft is so subtle and difficult to detect that God answered by fire in order to make the true power of God glaringly obvious. Elijah stated, "If I am a man of God…"

In the days of Moses the prophet, Korah, Dathan, and Abiram rose up (rebelled) before Moses, together with some of the Israelites, 250 leaders of the congregation chosen in the assembly, and men of distinction. They assembled together against Moses and Aaron to falsely accuse them. In turn, Moses challenged the counterfeit by putting conditions on the test to prove the authentic. He said to Korah and all his followers,

> In the morning the LORD will show who belongs to him, who is holy, and who it is that he will allow to come near him. Only the person the LORD chooses will be allowed to come near him. (Num. 16:5)

Once again, God used fire to distinguish between the true prophet and the impostor. After advising the people against such actions, fire came down from heaven to consume them:

> And fire came out from the LORD and consumed the 250 men who were offering the incense. (Num. 16:35)

In both examples aforementioned, God's fire consumed the veils that blinded the people's hearts so that they could plainly identify the one true God. In addition, He will do the same with His two witnesses in the end. The fire of God, which is His Word, will emanate from their mouths to utterly destroy all who try to oppose them in any way. They will be allotted a certain amount of time (three and a half years) to deliver their testimonies, and God will grant them the authority to speak with a burning zeal (fire) that will utterly destroy the chains of darkness and every every evil work encountered along the way.

God uses the element of fire for two main reasons: to burn the idols out of a man's heart and to separate (divide) the two kingdoms of light and darkness. For example, notice the correlation between fire and separation (division):

> Jesus said, "I came to bring fire on the earth, and how I wish it were already set ablaze! Do you think that I came here to give peace to the earth? No, I tell you, but rather division!" (Luke 12:49, 51)

Jesus's purpose for appearing on the earth was to bring fire. Jesus understood the importance of fire. Fire causes a division as it distinctly separates the wheat from the tares, the silver from the dross. As the end draws nearer, God will use His fire to separate His people from the idols in the land so they will not be judged with the ungodly. Jesus taught more about why it would be necessary for the separation of light and darkness, especially as it pertains to the end:

> Let both [weeds and wheat] grow together until the harvest. At that time I will tell the harvesters: First collect the weeds and tie them in bundles to be burned; then gather the wheat and bring it into my barn. (Matt. 13:30)

Jesus is coming back for people who have separated themselves from those who are wandering in Babylon. God's fire is healing, purifying fire used for separating man from his idols.

> For he [Jesus] will be like a blazing fire that refines metal, or like a strong soap that bleaches clothes. He will sit like a refiner of silver, burning away the dross. (Mal. 3:2–3)

The fire of God destroys the devil's work (1 John 3:8). Jesus's appearance on earth would kindle a burning fire within the heart of man, thus creating hostility within the kingdom of darkness and those who chose to remain in its blackness. Jesus understood this truth, saying, "My appearance to the earth brings division." This doesn't imply that Jesus was not a peacemaker. Indeed, he demonstrated a ministry of reconciliation and peace. He was the author of true peace, not as the world gives, but the peace of God that passes all human understanding. The Holy Ghost fire upon Jesus created hostility from an opposing kingdom of darkness. As a result, men gnashed their teeth at Him. Jesus brought the fire of God's heavenly kingdom to the earth. His presence is an all-consuming fire, mercifully burning the idols out of a man's heart in order that he may escape the eternal fire of hell's torment. God's fire is loving, merciful, yet all-consuming. His fire is holy and true. Its heat will refine a man, removing the dross (impurities) from the silver. In turn, this caused a division between the two fires: God's holy, preserving, sanctifying fire and hell's fiery torment. Some opposed this refining fire as they loved their idols more than God. Others, on the other hand, would choose the gospel of light. The appearance of Jesus on the earth meant war to the hosts of darkness as the opposing kingdom would pose a threat to the seed of destruction.

God is still using fire to consume Babylon's idols. In Deuteronomy, He instructed His creation to make the right choice: "Choose life!"

> Today I have given you the choice between life and death, between blessings and curses. Now I call on heaven and earth to witness the choice you make. Oh, that you would choose life, so that you and your descendants might live! (Deut. 30:19)

The stage is set, and the time is fast approaching when the two witnesses will make their appearance. They will pour out the golden oil from themselves and to the Church—the oil symbolizing the revelation knowledge of God's kingdom secrets. The Church should clearly understand the roles of the two witnesses so she doesn't get destroyed by the fire of God that emanates from their mouths. Indeed, they will be releasing judgment upon the idols in the land, but their works, as unmerciful as they may be seen to the wicked, will not be derived from within themselves. Instead, they are merciful acts of deliverance from a God who is still parting the Red Sea and proclaiming through His prophets, "Let my people go!"

For the people who are wandering around in the outskirt lands of Babylon, come out of your witchcrafts and support the judgments of God against those who stand up to defy and oppose the kingdom expansion, lest you be destroyed by the plagues that will be released by God's two end-time prophets.

When the Counterfeit Hits a Wall

Scriptures in Revelation 11 reveal that the two persons (witnesses) who are chosen to be the prophets of God in the last hour will have the power to turn water into blood.

> These are the two olive trees and the two lamp-stands standing before the God of the earth. And if anyone wants to harm them, fire proceeds from their mouth and devours their enemies. And if anyone wants to harm them, he must be killed in this manner. These have power to shut heaven, so that no rain falls in the days of their prophecy; and they have power over waters to turn them to blood, and to strike the earth with all plagues, as often as they desire. (Rev. 11:4–6)

Again, notice that the end-time prophets of Revelation 11 are given power during the reign of their prophecy to turn water into blood, much like the prophet Moses when he was up against the stouthearted Egyptian pharaoh.

> Moses and Aaron did as the LORD commanded. In the sight of Pharaoh and in the sight of his servants he lifted up the staff and struck the water in the Nile, and all the water in the Nile turned into blood. (Exod. 7:20)

During that time, the fish in the Nile died and the river smelled so bad the Egyptians couldn't drink the water. Blood was everywhere in Egypt.

The two witnesses in the end will be given power in the same manner when up against the witchcraft kingdom that withstands their testimony of Jesus. The counterfeit power of witchcraft in Egypt entangled the people of God in Moses's day, and it will seek to do the same in the end when the two witnesses stand before the earth to administer judgment during that time.

According to tradition, two of the magicians who were summoned by the Egyptian pharaoh to oppose Moses were Jannes and Jambres.

The Bible doesn't offer much information about Jannes and Jambres. As a matter of fact, these two are only mentioned one time "by name" in the entire Bible, and they show up in the New Testament. Describing the wickedness of the last days, Paul says,

> Just as Jannes and Jambres opposed Moses, so also these men oppose the truth. They are depraved and disqualified from the faith. But they will not advance much further. For just like Jannes and Jambres, their folly will be plain to everyone. (2 Tim. 3:8–9)

Although their names are not mentioned in the book of Exodus 7, Jewish tradition claims that Jannes and Jambres were the two chief magicians in Egypt who withstood Moses and Aaron during the time of the plagues.

> Aaron threw his staff down in front of Pharaoh and his officials, and it became a snake. Pharaoh then summoned wise men and sorcerers, and the Egyptian magicians also did the same things by their secret arts: Each one threw down his staff and it became a snake. But Aaron's staff swallowed their staffs. (Exod. 7:10–12)

Later, these same sorcerers also duplicated two of God's other plagues of Egypt: the changing of water into blood (Exod. 7:22) and the production of frogs (Exod. 8:7). However, they were not able to duplicate the remaining plagues through the use of their magic (Exod. 8:19). This goes to show that there will always come a time when the counterfeit will be exposed. As the truth continues to move forward, it separates itself from the false, clearly leaving it behind as an imitation. This is when the counterfeit is made manifest, exposed as an impostor.

Paul used the wickedness and defiance of Jannes and Jambres (through their acts of witchcraft) to illustrate the presence of a wide-spread rejection of the truth in the last days.

Witchcraft doesn't always deny the existence of the power of God outrightly; it simply tries to imitate it. Through imitation, Jannes and Jambres depreciated the value of the real thing as Satan uses the counterfeit to damage people's confidence in the truth. In the eye of the undiscerning, it can almost be impossible to tell the difference between the truth and the counterfeit because these things are spiritually discerned (1 Cor. 2:14), imperceptible to the natural eye. As a matter of fact, the word *occult* means "hidden, difficult to see, imperceptible to the eye."

Jannes and Jambres's attempts to diminish the genuine power of God by using imitation (witchcraft) proved to be an utter failure. The power of the Jannes and Jambres spirit does more to paralyze the testimony of the Church than all the persecution that it has ever met, seeing that outright persecution and acts of injustice actually breed revival. Remaining obscure as a counterfeit is not so obvious.

According to the Bible, witchcraft is the work of a covert thief. Jude wrote about this kind: "These men are the hidden reefs in your love feasts, shamelessly feasting with you..." (Jude 1:12).

They are hidden because they are of the Jannes and Jambres occultic spirit.

Paul said that Jannes and Jambres opposed Moses, just as men in the last days will stand up and defiantly oppose the truth (2 Tim. 3:8).

The word *oppose* in this verse is the Greek word *anthístēmi* (*antí* meaning "opposite/against" and *hístēmi*, "to stand")—properly, to take a complete stand against (i.e., a "180 degree, contrary position"), and figuratively, to establish one's position publicly by conspicuously "holding one's ground" and refusing to be moved ("pushed back"). The word *anthístēmi* was actually a military term in classical Greek meaning "to strongly resist an opponent" ("take a firm stand against").

Paul said that the minds of these impostors would be depraved. The word *depraved* in this verse in Greek is *kataphtheírō* (*katá* meaning "down," *phtheírō* meaning "corrupt")—properly, corrupted all the way down (thoroughly degenerated), utterly corrupted. This refers to a man who has so yielded himself to works of unrighteousness that he has been despoiled and brought down to a lower (inferior) form, a degenerate.

This is such a wretched condition for a man to be in, especially as he *continues* to oppose the truth. The Jannes and Jambres spirit is the same occultic (counterfeit) spirit of the end. This is the spirit of the lawless one (the Antichrist) and all who choose to follow him. Scriptures in the book of Revelation indicate that the beast will do miracles so that the world will believe him.

> He did astounding miracles, even making fire flash down to earth from the sky while everyone was watching. And with all the miracles he was allowed to perform on behalf of the first beast, he deceived all the people who belong to this world. He ordered the people to make a great statue of the first beast, who was fatally wounded and then came back to life. He was then permitted to give life to this statue so that it could speak. Then the statue of the beast commanded that anyone refusing to worship it must die. He required everyone—small and great, rich and poor, free and slave—to be given a mark on the right hand or on the forehead. And no one could buy or sell

> anything without that mark, which was either the
> name of the beast or the number representing his
> name. Wisdom is needed here. Let the one with
> understanding solve the meaning of the number
> of the beast, for it is the number of a man. His
> number is 666. (Rev. 13:13–18)

These miracles will be performed using a counterfeit "witch-craft" power. The world will believe it to be the truth. However, the good news is this: it will be just as Paul predicted in his letter to Timothy.

> But they will not advance much further. For just
> like Jannes and Jambres, their folly will be plain
> to everyone. (2 Tim. 3:8–9)

Although the powers of witchcraft might make some headway, it will not advance much further when there is a "Moses" present. The powers of darkness will not be able to fully duplicate God's powers in the end.

First Kings 4:30 says, "Solomon's wisdom surpassed the wisdom of all the people of the east and all the wisdom of Egypt."

This verse indicates that Solomon's wisdom *surpassed* all the other wisdom. The truth of God will continue but the counterfeit will fizzle out. God's wisdom "exceeds" when Satan's wisdom hits a wall.

Jannes and Jambres could only get so far using counterfeit (witchcraft) powers. They were not able to duplicate the power of God for the remaining plagues.

> The magicians tried to produce gnats using their
> magic arts, but they could not. And the gnats
> remained on man and beast. (Exod. 8:18)

As a result of their inability to produce the same miracles as Moses, the magicians said to Pharaoh, "This is the finger of God!

But Pharaoh's heart remained hard. He wouldn't listen to them, just as the LORD had predicted" (verse 19).

Under what conditions does a man find himself operating in the Jannes and Jambres spirit? Paul said, "They are depraved in mind and disqualified from the faith" (2 Tim. 3:8).

As far as the faith is concerned, they are rejected or disqualified. The word *disqualified* is the Greek word *adokimos*, which means that they have failed to pass the test. They have not been approved because they were unable to stand the test. Why? Because there came a day when the storms of this life tested the foundation of everything they were building their lives on. Sadly, their building endeavors were in vain, and everything their hands had constructed came crashing down. They denied the refining wilderness test that God offers for purification and, instead, chose to be self-sufficient throughout their lives. Their own personal choices caused them to become disqualified.

The *Strong's Concordance* referred to this type of person as a moral castaway. In this form of the word, a *castaway* is "one who is ruined, one who has made a moral shipwreck, a reprobate." Since he failed the test, he is deemed a counterfeit because he remains unpruned and unrefined. Hence, he has been unapproved and is disqualified to carry God's glory.

In the end, when a person is not a vessel of truth, they are a part of the counterfeit. The powers operating through them are not truth from God but counterfeit, because they have been deemed "unfit." These are people who desire power without paying the price. The price that one must pay is to lay his own life down for the kingdom of God and His righteousness.

Although the powers of witchcraft are actively operating in our world today, there will come a time when the impostors will be exposed. Paul writes, "For just like Jannes and Jambres, their folly will be plain to everyone" (2 Tim. 3:9).

The Lord will indefinitely expose these impostors. He will manifest all things that are hidden. These deceivers, whose goal is to remain covert in operation, will be made completely obvious to all men: "Their folly will be made plain to everyone."

The word *folly* in this verse is linked to rage and bitterness. *Folly* in Greek is *ánoia* (from a privative meaning "no" and *noús*, meaning "mind")—properly, "no mind," referring to a person of irrational behavior and mindless actions. They have a "lack of sense," which easily degenerates into "a state of extreme anger that suggests an incapacity to use their mind due to an extreme fury and great rage" (*Strong's Concordance*).

Evidently, those who work witchcraft are so consumed with bitterness that their fury will be revealed and made obvious to all men. Through their violent outbursts, they will prove their instability.

The kingdom of witchcraft is highly competitive against the power of God. Workers of iniquity become enraged as they stand up to defy the armies of God.

However, light will always expose darkness. The brighter the light, the greater the exposure. For the Jannes and Jambres spirit to be revealed in this end-time, we must be a *Moses* who has been found worthy (qualified) to carry the power of God to a pharaoh or one who reigns over the end-time Babylonian kingdom of witchcraft. Just like Jannes and Jambres, workers of iniquity will hit a wall as they oppose the power of God working through you. They will not be able to duplicate the miracles of the Creator of miracles! As a result, you will have the testimony of Daniel. Scriptures say,

> In every matter of wisdom and understanding about which the king questioned them, the king found Daniel's wisdom ten times better than all the magicians and enchanters in his whole kingdom. (Dan. 1:20)

As the two witnesses come to the forefront to commence their ministries, the Jannes and Jambres spirit will subtly seek to undermine the workings of the Holy Ghost through them in an attempt to destroy their work. Their works will be their fruits that are used to benefit the wounded souls of others. This spirit will aggressively form satanic weapons to discredit their testimonies by sabotaging them personally. When the counterfeit power sees it's no match for the power of God within God's two prophets, vindictive men of the wicked nature will seek to humiliate them, their families, and their reputations. However, the folly of the wicked will be made plain for all to behold. The counterfeit powers will hit a wall, and the oil that is secreted from the two witnesses will be used for the lanterns of the Church to bring light. Then the body of Christ will see and know what is truth and what is false.

The Beast from the Bottomless Pit

Revelation 11 reveals that just after the two witnesses complete their testimonies, the beast will arise from the bottomless pit to wage war against God's two end-time prophets, eventually killing them.

> When they finish their testimony, the beast that ascends out of the bottomless pit will make war against them, overcome them, and kill them. (Rev. 11:7)

According to the *Strong's Concordance*, the figurative beast (the Greek word *thérion*), depicted as the Antichrist, refers to a man whose nature transforms into something bestial and animalistic.

How does a person's nature transform from a man to a beast? What does the process of this transformation look like? The Antichrist, the man, will be possessed by a beast spirit from Satan's animal kingdom. The actual entity that possesses him will come from the underworld. It is specifically assigned for this end-time role and will be released only at the command of God in His set/appointed time.

The beast spirit (*thérion*) comes from *théra*, which means "to hunt or to entrap, a prey, a game, a net, a means of capture" (*Strong's Concordance*). Therefore, this is the way it all ends for God's two Revelation 11 prophets. They will be hunted and entrapped like prey when it is captured in a hunter's net.

My Dream of a Beast

I'll never forget one particular late-night trip to the store a few years ago. I was scanning my items through self-check when I saw three men enter the store. Immediately I perceived in my spirit that they were spiritually dark. However, I was not prepared for what was about to transpire. They quickly picked up an item and entered the self-check section where I was. As they drew closer, I made eye contact with each of them. Although they all possessed gross spiritual darkness, two of the three looked ordinary to the natural eye. However, when the man in the middle smiled at me, I no longer saw a human face. Instead, he transformed into a hairy black beast with a distorted mouth of a scoffer. That's the only way I can describe it. I am certain that no one else around me that night saw what I saw. God was allowing me to catch a glimpse of this horrific transformation because He would use it as a lesson for me to share with others.

The sight seemed unimaginable, the present darkness bone-chilling. I blinked my eyes to make sure I was seeing correctly. I'm not going to lie, I was creeped out. It's not an everyday occurrence for a human face to be overshadowed by a demon spirit. Yet God allowed my natural eyes to perceive the spiritual darkness that existed within this person. Had this man known that the monstrous entity who disfigured his face and possessed his soul looked this repulsive, he would be terrified.

The hair stood up on my arms as I rushed to load my bags into the cart. When I closed the car door, I questioned God, "What was it that my eyes just witnessed?" I heard the Spirit of God speak within me, "Those men are walking in darkness, and you perceived it within yourself. However, the one whose image transformed had a spiritual walk that was deeper into the occult. He had a dark 'kingdom' in him."

How does a man become a beast, and at what juncture does this transformation occur within the Antichrist in the book of Revelation?

Nebuchadnezzar Transforms into a Beast

An example of this type of man-to-beast transformation can be found in Daniel 4. Nebuchadnezzar, king of Babylon, tells of his vision of an angelic messenger who came down from heaven with the judgment of God upon him:

> Let his [Nebuchadnezzar's] heart be changed from man's, and let a beast's heart be given unto him; and let seven times [years] pass over him. (Dan. 4:16)

Nebuchadnezzar had become a mighty man on the earth. He had made the statement as he looked out across the city:

> Look at this great city of Babylon! By my own mighty power, I have built this beautiful city as my royal residence to display my majestic splendor. (Dan. 4:30)

Because of Nebuchadnezzar's pride and self-exaltation, God allowed his heart to be changed from a man's to that of a beast. So extreme was this transformation that he was driven away from humanity for seven years and into the wild to live with the beasts of the field. He was made to eat grass like cattle till his hair had grown like eagles' feathers and his nails like birds' claws. After the demonic spirit of a beast entered him, his whole nature changed, from that of a man to the demon spirit that now possessed him.

In like manner, I believe that the man I saw in the store that night had the heart of a beast, just like the story of Nebuchadnezzar's transformation.

The Antichrist Becomes a Beast

This is the same "beast spirit" that will enter the Antichrist at the end of time. The word *beast* (*thērion*) in the book of Revelation is always used in reference to a person, the future Antichrist (or his system). The man alone is *the Antichrist;* the man possessed with a brute spirit becomes *the beast,* hence the meaning behind the metamorphosis into a hybrid (part human, part animal).

As Nebuchadnezzar's heart transformed from a man's to that of a beast, in like manner, the Antichrist as man will transform into *the beast*. As a matter of fact, we can pinpoint the exact time this is first mentioned in scripture.

> Now when they [God's two witnesses] have finished their testimony, the beast that comes up from the Abyss will attack them, and overpower and kill them. (Rev. 11:7)

This is not a reference here to a metaphysical spirit who murders God's two prophets in the end but a man possessed by a beast spirit from Satan's animal kingdom. As the two witnesses wrap up their end-time ministries, a ruling spirit will be released from the bottomless pit and will enter the Antichrist (Rev. 9:11, Rev. 11:7). The Antichrist, therefore, becomes the beast. He will become brutish and violent in nature as he is compelled to destroy God's two prophets, but not before they complete their testimonies. The beast described in Revelation 13—although he has *many* horns, crowns, and heads—is still only one man. Notice in the verses below how often the beast is referred to as *him*:

> And they worshipped the beast, saying, Who is like unto the beast? who is able to make war with him? And there was given unto him a mouth speaking great things and blasphemies; and power was given unto him to continue forty and two months. (Rev. 13:4–5)

Evidently, then, it will be a mortal man who will be speaking, ruling, and walking in power while on earth, not a disembodied being. He will be a leader of a kingdom composed of a conglomeration of tribes, nations, and people. Notice in the verse above that he is given a mouth to speak great things and blasphemies. In my personal experience, I believe the man I saw transform in the store that night had the same blasphemous mouth—that of a scoffer. And just as Nebuchadnezzar was using his mouth to boast of great things concerning himself and his kingdom, the beast (Antichrist) of the end will be given a mouth that speaks great, swelling words and blasphemies. Paul writes,

> He will oppose and will exalt himself over everything that is called God or is worshipped, so that he sets himself up in God's temple, proclaiming himself to be God. (2 Thess. 2:4)

These are the main characteristics of the *man-beast* in the last days. After the demonic spirit of a beast enters him, he transforms into something terrible in nature and begins to use his mouth to boast great things about himself. The examples in the verse aforementioned describe the spiritual transformation from man to beast after his soul becomes demon-possessed.

Process of Becoming a Mighty Man on Earth

Another example of man-to-beast transformation is found in the account of Nimrod. The book of Genesis reveals how fallen angels began to have sexual relations with women (Gen. 6:3). As a result, humans gave birth to children from these angels. Their offspring, then, were part human, part demon, also called Nephilim or giants. The whole earth (the human race) began to be filled with those who were of the seed of Satan (Nephilim, "giants") (Gen. 6). This offspring would rise to become tyrants in the land who would hunt the human race, subdue the righteous seed, and overtake it. Nimrod and Esau were just two who exemplified the characteristics of the *hunter spirit* that possessed them. Genesis 10:9 says, "He [Nimrod] became a mighty hunter in defiance of the LORD. That is why it is said (the proverb), "Like Nimrod, a mighty hunter in defiance of the LORD."

Notice the words *he became*, which entails a progression into becoming something different. Nimrod, a carrier of the seed of Cain and the grandson of Ham, would *become* one of these mighty men of the earth in those days. This is indicative of a transformation into becoming someone who was mighty on the earth. Nimrod began to display some of the very same characteristics of a hunter. Most likely, within his *spiritual* DNA was the seed of the giants who had risen in those days. Scriptures say that he progressed into someone *mighty*.

The word *mighty* in Hebrew is *gibbor*, which is defined as "a champion, a chief, excel, a giant, a man, a mighty man, one [tyrant], a strong man" (*Strong's Concordance*). These giants of old *became* mighty men. This is in reference to one who magnifies himself and behaves proudly, a tyrant who is bold and audacious. These men rose to power as they continued in iniquity. This also entails a transformation into deeper darkness, which Revelation 2:24 refers to as Satan's so-called deep secrets. This esoteric knowledge pushed them to the forefront and gave them *hunting* powers to influence, conquer, defile, and slay the righteous seed.

How does a person transform from a man into a beast? What does this process (transformation) look like? Spiritual bondage involves a slow fade away from the truth. A person gives pieces of himself away for a heavy price. In this life, he makes choices, either bad or good. If these choices are repeated long enough, they turn into habits that become automatic. In other words, over time, a person stops battling the urge to oppose the thing he should deny. Once habits are formed, he naturally begins to identify with the addictions. At this point, he has allowed his actions to characterize who he is as a person. This is the manner in which a person's nature changes. Therefore, there are *stages of evil* a person undergoes before a complete metamorphosis occurs, much like the Egyptian pharaoh as he continued to harden his heart against God. The heart can become adamantine when a person ignores the inner promptings of the Lord. Zechariah 7:12 says, "They made their hearts as hard as flint so that they couldn't hear the LORD's teachings…"

In the Bible, James writes about the progressive stages of sin and parallels it to conception, growth, maturation, and birth:

> But each person is tempted by his own desire,
> being lured and trapped by it. When lust becomes

pregnant, it gives birth to sin; and when that sin
grows up, it gives birth to death. (James 1:14–15)

There are progressive stages of prenatal development. The degrees of evil are likened to the *stages* of prenatal development and the eventual *birth* of an infant.

Sin, like lust, will reach maturation if it's continually fed. Once our standards are lowered, we forfeit our defenses as we sow seeds of compromise. As time evolves, it becomes easier to grab a piece of fruit that dangles from the tree of divination. So often we stop fighting off urges because the hidden sin has become a way of life. As a result, when sin reaches maturation, it gives birth to death.

A thorough transformation occurs when a man's nature changes. It means he is now suffering from an identity crisis because he more closely relates to a lower form of existence.

In our society today exists an identity phenomenon called therianthropy, in which certain individuals feel that they are in some way and to some degree beasts (animals).

The word *therianthropy* comes from the combined Greek words *thérion*, which means "wild beast," and *anthropos*, meaning "human" ("part human, part beast"). In parallel, the word *beast* in the book of Revelation is also *thérion* in Greek.

For a person to consider themself a beast (animal) would entail an extreme identity crisis and would be the ultimate insult to their Creator. Psalm 8:4–8 states, "What is man that You are mindful of him…? For You have made him a little lower than the angels, And You have crowned him with glory and honor. You have made him to have dominion over the works of Your hands; You have put all *things* under his feet, All sheep and oxen—Even the beasts of the field, The birds of the air, And the fish of the sea That pass through the paths of the seas."

According to the previous verse, man has been given dominion *over* the beast (animal) kingdom: "You have put all things under his feet."

God made man to be like Him, not like a beast. Genesis 5:1 says, "When God created man, he made him in the likeness of God."

Is it any wonder why Satan would work hard to engender an identity crisis within the human race? If God's creation perceives themselves to be on the level of a beast, they will not walk in the dominion (authority) that subdues Satan's earthly kingdoms.

Jesus has commanded us to trample on snakes and scorpions (Luke 10:19). He was speaking in metaphors, however, in an attempt to convey that God's created man should be walking in an authority above every form and level of darkness. In addition, how is a man going to assume a position above a beast or an animal if he believes he is one?

In like manner, scriptures indicate that Satan himself has the ability to transform in various ways, as we have learned from the story in the garden where he embodied a serpent. In his letter to the Corinthians, Paul mentioned these transformations and how Satan's human instruments also have the ability to transform themselves:

> These people are false apostles. They are deceitful workers who *transform themselves* as apostles of Christ. And no wonder! For Satan himself *transforms himself* into an angel of light. So it is no wonder that his servants also *transform themselves* as servants of righteousness. In the end they will get the punishment their wicked deeds deserve. (2 Cor. 11:13–15)

There is a phenomenon within Satanism that encourages a person to "reclaim the beast" within themselves. As a matter of fact, the man-to-beast transformation is a core belief of Satanism. Furthermore, many manuals have been written by Satanists, giving instructions for becoming a werewolf (called lycanthropy). These are books that contain information about the transformation from an ordinary man to a warlock and how the warlock identifies with the wolf in all its masculinity and cunning. Many Satanists teach that civilized human qualities regress and become more animalistic under emotional stress.

This is an incredible lowering of the human form into Satan's animal (beast) kingdom, a powerless transformation indeed. The Church must know her place above the powers of darkness so that her members can walk in the authority to loosen the bands of wickedness, undo the heavy burdens, let the oppressed go free, and break the yokes from those who are enslaved to these debased beliefs.

People of this nature occupy leadership positions and own their own businesses. They are walking the streets, lining up in the grocery aisles, and could possibly be living in our own homes. They are raising children and teaching other people's children at school. Although these subjects need to be delivered out of Satan's grip, the members of Christ's body must be operating in the power of God to subdue the kingdoms of darkness so that Satan's human instruments cannot infect the human race any longer. They are offspring of Satan from the reptilian (serpent) kingdom and will continue in mischief and witchcraft so long as they are benefitting from their sorceries and manipulations.

The truth about deception can be found in Romans 12. In his letter to the Romans, Paul writes, "Do not conform to the pattern of this world, but be transformed by the renewing of your mind" (Rom. 12:2).

Here, Paul warns us to not conform to the thought patterns of the world. The word *conform* is *suschématizó*, which means "to assume a similar *outward form* [expression] by following the worldly pattern [model, mold]." The first part of the word, *sýn*, means "identify with" and *sxēmatizō* means "having outward shape."

This explanation is so befitting. The word *conform* in this verse so accurately describes the man-to-beast transformation process and where it begins. For anyone to identify himself with a creature, a beast, or any animal within the beast kingdom, it first began in the mind, following the world's system of thought. Paul said not to "conform" to those thoughts about yourself. Just because something feels to be real in your mind doesn't mean that it is. Remember, Satan is a shapeshifter. He has the ability to transform himself into an angel of light. Scriptures indicate that he is the "father of all lies." If a man conforms to believing a particular thing about himself, he will soon identify with the image that has been constructed within his imagination about who he is. Through this process, he is allowing Satan to invent another mind within him (a double-minded man is a man of two minds/souls). This is how two separate minds within a single individual are created and explains why *shifts* from one form into another might occur (the meaning behind *conform* (*sxēmatizō*), "having outward shape").

Beware of programs or organizations that offer progressive or transformational stages (degrees) of power and illumination (enlightenment)—such as Freemasonry, Satanism, paganism, Buddhism, etc.—sworn oaths, memberships, and affiliations within these organizations are sometimes how Satan gets an inlet (open door) into our family lineage to affect our offspring.

As opposed to *conforming* to the world, Paul encouraged us to be *transformed* by the renewing of our minds according to the Word of God (Rom. 12:2). This type of transformation, unlike the debasement involved in conforming to the world, is not a transformation into a werewolf, vampire, beast, or animal but is God's authentic purpose of transformation, which in no way debases God's created man.

The word *transform*, which is by God's Word, comes from *metamorphoó* which is defined as "metamorphize, change, and transfigure." This transformation entails a change in the form that comes *after being with*. As we spend time soaking ourselves in God's Word, we are altered in various ways for the betterment of who we were created to become. God is never going to lower His people to a bestial form considering that He creates human masterpieces that reveal His glory and splendor (Gen. 1:27, Ps. 139:14).

As for those of us who are living in the last days, when the son of perdition (2 Thess. 2:3) becomes possessed by the beast spirit that is released from the abyss, may we have the discernment to know the authentic from the counterfeit. The two witnesses will be operating in the office of a prophet. They will be explaining the prophetic signs of the times and revealing the secrets of the kingdom. Their ministry will also involve judging Babylon (Satan's spiritual kingdoms that enslave mankind on earth) and her children (those who drink from Babylon's cup). The beast will become enraged, and the two witnesses will finally lay down their lives and willingly submit to martyrdom. Their blood, which will be spilled onto the soil of the earth, and their bodies, which will serve as seed for the Church, will strengthen the souls of the wayward. It will be a glorious day, as three and a half days later, God's two anointed ones will be resurrected before their persecutors. They will be caught up in a cloud and swept away, alive forevermore.

The Two Who Bring Oil

Although the Bible only refers to the "two witnesses" as such in Revelation 11, chances are, the Church has failed to see that these two prophets were spoken of in Zechariah 3 and 4 and alluded to again in one of Jesus's parables, the ten virgins. That's right. Although they may go unrecognized in other parts of the Bible, the Church body's starring cast in the tribulation, the two witnesses, are actually mentioned in the Bible as far back as the Old Testament and in one of Jesus's New Testament parables.

Through parables, Jesus illustrated the nature of things just before His return. One of the most insightful stories He used to reveal the state of the Church in the end is the parable of the ten virgins.

Since the parable of the ten virgins spoke concerning the end of times, Jesus conveyed that He would raise up prophets in the last days to help the unprepared subjects (virgins) "purchase the oil" (see Matt. 25:9). Two of the prophets, more specifically, are the Revelation 11 duo who rise up at the appointed time to encourage the Church, reveal her poor condition, and teach her the authority that comes with having the testimony of Jesus.

What does the oil in the parable of the virgins represent, and how is it related to the two witnesses who will be distributing it to the world in the last days?

Scriptures reveal that God will raise up two people, alive during that time, who will have global end-time ministries. Perhaps they are alive even now, but only God will appoint the proper time for them to step to the forefront. They are referred to as the two witnesses or the two olive trees mentioned in Revelations 11, also known as the two who bring oil. In John's vision, God revealed that the two olive trees were emblematic of two prophets who would arise at the end of the age and pour oil into the lamps to give light to the seven churches (candlesticks) (Rev. 1:11, 20).

Centuries prior to John's vision in the book of Revelation, God had also given the Old Testament prophet Zechariah a glimpse of these two end-time prophets (metaphorically) who would bring oil to the earth. The prophet Zechariah inquired about the two olive trees in the vision:

> Then I said to him, "What are these two olive trees on the right of the lampstand and on its left?" And I answered the second time and said to him, "What are the two olive branches which are beside the two golden pipes, which empty the golden *oil* from themselves?" So he answered me, saying, "Do you not know what these are?" And I said, "No, my lord." Then he said, "These are the two anointed ones who are standing by the Lord of the whole earth." (Zech. 4:11–14)

Let's zoom in on the last verse where it reads, "These are the two anointed ones" (verse 14). If you notice in the footnotes, the Hebrew translates this to say, "The two who bring fresh oil."

It is evident that the two persons mentioned in Zechariah 3 and 4 are the same two witnesses in Revelations 11 who will appear at the end of times. These two will appear before the world, and they will be anointed to "bring oil" to the Church so that it may have light to openly see again. While it's important to have a lamp in this dispensation of gross spiritual darkness, it's equally important to have the oil that goes along with the lamp. The lamp, only if it has a supply of oil, will give light.

The Church of the last days will need light to see by so she can commence her journey to meet the Bridegroom (in the air) (1 Thess. 4:17). That's right. She is not to merely wait but to search for Him until she meets Him face-to-face. Jesus begins the parable by saying,

> At that time the kingdom of heaven will be like
> ten virgins who took their lamps and went out to
> meet the bridegroom. (Matt. 25:1)

Notice that the virgins grabbed their lamps, and "they went out." This entails that we, too, are travelers who will be in pursuit of Him when He appears.

> For here we have no lasting city, but we seek the
> city that is to come. (Heb. 13:14)

There is action involved on our part in seeking our permanent residence. The Church has failed to perceive that the parable of the ten virgins is a depiction of a spiritual journey she will have to make if she is going to "meet the Bridegroom," which is Jesus, upon His arrival. A wedding has been scheduled, and the bride (the Church) will need to be dressed, ready, and "on her way" to the wedding ceremony.

Our spiritual journey here on earth, then, is characterized by progressive stages of forward movement: "Ask, seek, and knock" (Matt. 7:7). Proverbs 4:18 says, "The road the righteous travel is like the sunrise, getting brighter and brighter until daylight has come."

Indeed, we are *traveling* on a road that is bringing us closer to the magnificent lights of our permanent home in the glorious realm.

Our innate desire should be to seek this perfect place (Heb. 13:14) that does actually exist in order to permanently settle with our Creator.

I had a dream once where my dad and I were in a vehicle traveling to a large city that was set atop a hill. The city shone with magnificent lights, but the road that led into the city was very dark and winding. I could see that we were miles and miles in distance from the city, but we were traveling toward it. My dad was driving, and I was in the passenger seat giving him directions. The darkness was so great and the path so obscure that I kept telling him to slow down and watch the bending curves. I believe this entails the believer's spiritual journey toward the heavenly city.

The road we travel is like the rising of the sun in the morning; the more revelation knowledge we receive, the closer we get to "the city" and the brighter our path becomes along our journey. Paul referred to our journey toward God as an upward call. In that case, then, the direction we travel to meet the bridegroom is more of an ascension as we rise to the higher regions of the glorious realms (Phil. 3:14).

In the story of the ten virgins, Matthew 25:1 indicates that all ten had commenced their journeys: "They went forth to meet the bridegroom."

In addition, all ten had their lamps in hand, according to the first verse. It is pretty self-explanatory here that the lamp referenced in the parable is the Word of God that has the ability (when imparted) to reveal (or bear light), as lamps do. Psalm 119:105 says, "Your word is a lamp to my feet and a light to my path." However, the lamp will only reveal light when coupled with oil just as the Word will only impart newness and create the miraculous when it is anointed by the Holy Ghost.

Evidently, all ten virgins brought their lamps with them. However, as the parable suggests, just because a person carries their lamp, or Bible, under their arm doesn't necessarily signify they will be ready when the bridegroom appears.

Jesus chose ten virgins to represent the two categories of people that would exist in the end: those who were *prepared* and those who were *unprepared* for Christ's return. Hence, the meaning behind why five were *wise* and the other five were *foolish*. This is proof that many within the body of Christ will not be walking in the light upon His return. Therefore, Jesus deems them "foolish" and "unprepared" for His return.

A distinct separation exists between the two groups. A person will either be among the *wise* or the *foolish*, no middle ground. Additionally, there will only be one reason for the line of demarcation that exists between the two categories of people, and that is the oil. Some will have it; others won't.

"The foolish ones took their lamps but did not take any oil with them. The wise ones, however, took oil in jars along with their lamps."

I believe that the *jars* in this verse are a reference to the compartments of a man's spirit. We are the containers mentioned in this verse. We contain the oil only if we house God's power within us, but sadly, many Christians don't. In his letter to the Corinthians, Paul writes,

> We are like clay jars in which this treasure is
> stored. The real power comes from God and not
> from us. (2 Cor. 4:7)

Man is the container of oil in this parable. If the anointing from within a man's spirit emerges as a continual flow of oil, he will have the light that is necessary for him to be able to see clearly enough to *complete* his journey, hence the meaning of the *extra oil* in the jars. It's impossible for a man to make a long journey in his car solely on the gasoline that's in the tank. He will need *additional* gas, beyond that which will only get him started on his journey.

Both the lamp and the oil are imperative for being able to see in the dark. However, the greater reason for having oil was for the *light* in order to see by. A lamp without oil will not give light, nor will oil without a lamp bring light. Both the lamp and the oil are required to manufacture the light.

When a person has the Word (lamp) but doesn't have the anointing of the Holy Ghost (oil), he will lack revelation knowledge (light). Paul said there would be many who would have a form of godliness, but they would "deny the power of God." Jeremiah 2:13 says that we deny His power by rejecting His Spirit (the oil) (John 7:38–39). As a result, the foolish virgins and those alike won't have the oil to sustain them down the straightaway.

A man can have a head knowledge of the Bible and thereby quote a great portion of what it says. The greater question is this: Has it been imparted, and does he have a revealed knowledge that illuminates his path to show him the way to the Father in this final hour?

In this parable, the foolish virgins looked up to find themselves short of oil, but by that time, it was too late to go buy any.

Jesus predicted that in the end, the Church would have the lamp (the Word), as was demonstrated among the ten virgins, but not all would necessarily have the oil (the power). We can turn on our TVs or tune in to any Christian radio station and hear good preaching, yet we are still not "seeing our signs." The power of God is not being demonstrated through the body of Christ (especially in our nation) through the gifts of the Spirit (the gift of healing, the gift of working miracles, etc.).

Jesus used the parable of the ten virgins to describe the time in which we now live. We lack oil, the anointing from His Spirit to do great and mighty things. It is through the miraculous that the world will know that God's Word does what it claims to do.

Paul explained in his letter to the Corinthians that he not only preached the Word but he also demonstrated what he taught through the signs and miracles that followed his ministry (1 Cor. 2:4). Paul knew not to separate the two (the lamp and the oil), for one without the other is "a broken cistern that can hold no water" (Jer. 2:13).

Jesus came as *the Word* made flesh (John 1:14), yet He was also anointed with *the Holy Ghost* power (Luke 4:18) to do great miraculous works. Therefore, during His ministry, the Word was confirmed with signs following. He was able to *demonstrate* the gospel and not just *talk about* its power. For that reason, the religious people, "the foolish," rejected Him for it! They had a form of godliness but denied the power. In other words, they rejected the oil.

As the parable goes on to reveal, the Groom arrived and the foolish were caught off guard. Matthew 25:6–9 says,

> In the middle of the night there was a shout: "Here's the groom! Come out to meet him." Then all the virgins got up and trimmed their lamps. The foolish ones said to the wise ones, "Give us some of your oil, because our lamps are going out." The wise [virgins] answered, "No, there won't be enough [oil] for us and for you.

Go instead to those who sell oil, and buy some
for yourselves."

When the bridegroom called, the lamps of the five foolish virgins began to sputter because of a shortage of oil. These five turned
to those who had oil and asked to freely take from theirs. The wise
virgins said, "No. Go and buy your own oil from those who sell it." I
believe that Jesus was trying to teach us a lesson here. There is a price
one has to pay for the oil, for the anointing of God to be operating
in their life. We can't just "borrow" our neighbor's relationship with
God or their knowledge of Him. Scriptures say "buy the truth," not
"borrow the truth." Furthermore, we will need both the lamp and
the oil upon Christ's return, which equates to having the wisdom and
knowledge that comes from the Word and the powerful anointing
that imparts (reveals) it.

By not being prepared, half the populace was about to miss the
wedding feast (eternal life).

How does one purchase the oil? The price that has to be paid
is the crucifixion of "self." Paul said, "I am crucified with Christ."
When Christ died, we died too. In this way, we should put to death
"self" so that Christ may be the one alive in us! Paul admonished the
Galatians,

> Now those who belong to Christ Jesus have cru-
> cified the flesh with its passions and desires. (Gal.
> 5:24)

Jesus said,

> If anyone wishes to come after me, he must deny
> himself, and take up his cross daily and follow
> me. (Luke 9:23)

This is most definitely the price that must be paid for the oil.
The process involved in refining our faith (buying the oil) is volun-

tary, but sadly, many choose the broader path that carries the least amount of resistance.

Through His parable of the virgins, Jesus acknowledged the fact that God would station "golden oil" suppliers for the lost.

Although the members of Christ's body should be producing the oil for those who are groping in darkness, the two witnesses will, on a large scale, be two of the golden oil vendors mentioned in the parable who administer the golden oil from themselves and to the world (Zech. 4:12).

They will have extra oil to sell in the end-time as they will have the insight and the anointing to impart *vision* and *revelation knowledge* to the Churches across the world. They will be on an assignment to open the eyes of the blind so that the body of Christ can find the narrow path to the Bridegroom. They will also have a ministry that reconciles the members of Christ's body together as one.

The heat that emanates from the fire of their testimonies, prophecies, and ministry will create a separation. It will have a sifting effect, removing Babylon's stumbling blocks. Their fire will burn the entire earth like a hot oven, causing the separation of the wheat and the tares to become more evident. Because of their ministries, the virgin bride of Christ will come out of Babylon, wash her robes, and arise to meet the Groom:

> Blessed are those who wash their robes, that they
> may have the right to the tree of life and may go
> through the gates into the city. (Rev. 22:14)

The Golden Oil

According to Zechariah 4, the two witnesses of the end will not only be bringing oil, but verse 12 indicates that they will be emptying "golden oil" out of themselves.

> What are the two olive branches which are beside
> the two golden pipes, which empty the golden oil
> from themselves? (Zech. 4:12)

From the previous chapter, we've learned that oil in the Bible is figurative for the Holy Ghost's power, which emanates from the human spirit to produce the miraculous signs here on earth. So then what is the meaning of the "golden" oil that will be emptied from the two witnesses in the last days?

Gold is the currency of heaven. It represents the precious (costly) things, such as our faith after it has endured the heat and been refined by the fiery trials.

As indicated before, walking in the anointing comes with a price that cannot be purchased with the currency of earth. The anointing can only be purchased with a heavenly currency, which is "gold" that is tried by fire.

In Revelation 3, God was speaking to the last-day Church when He said, "I advise you to buy from Me gold refined by fire so that you may become rich" (Rev. 3:18).

You may be thinking that this sounds strange; to buy anything from God just sounds off, but God is asking us to buy something from Him that will enlarge the borders of our hearts. A "gold that has been tried by fire" yields a refined faith that can change the world and the lost souls who are aimlessly wandering in it. Unfortunately, the faith of the Church has grown dreadfully weak. Jesus had concerns that upon His return, He might not find faith in the land. He asked the question, "When I return, will I find faith?" This proves that God is looking for one thing upon His return: faith.

Faith is only faith when it stands alone. Genuine faith that yields the golden oil cannot be produced without the fire component that filters out the impurities (fear, doubt, unbelief). The fire that tries our faith derives from the trials and tribulations we endure. For faith to be unmixed and unadulterated, it has to go through the refining process. It takes an unquestioning belief to offer God more of the compartments of our hearts. Crucifying the flesh requires us to lose all circumspection as we willfully make a choice to submit to God the unpliable regions of our hearts. The sacrifice we offer up to God that is most pleasing is when we "present our bodies as a living sacrifice" (Rom. 12:1, Heb. 11:6). Peter wrote,

> These trials will show that your faith is genuine.
> It [your faith] is being tested as fire tests and puri-
> fies gold—though your faith is far more precious
> than mere gold. (1 Pet. 1:7)

The golden oil is emblematic of an anointing that has been given to the two witnesses as a result of their faith being tested, refined, and proven by fire.

Revelation 11:3 says that in the days of their ministry, the two prophets will prophesy "clothed in sackcloth." Sackcloth was a coarse garment worn as a token of mourning by the Israelites. It was also a sign of submission (1 Kings 20:31–32) or of grief and self-humiliation (2 Kings 19:1) and was occasionally worn by the Hebrew prophets who led an austere life, such as John the Baptist (Matt. 3:4) and Elijah (2 Kings 1:8). The manner in which they dress could be taken literally or metaphorically. Either way, it is a sign to the world that the two prophets have endured the hardship that is required to become worthy of their calling. Like the great men of God that prevailed before them, they will have been hard-pressed and battle-tested before they ever take their places on the global scene. Satan is aware of the anointing that is upon the lives of God's two prophets, and we can be certain of this: their lives have been incessantly affected already by persecution from their adversaries, burdens too heavy to bear, mysterious illnesses in their physical bodies, etc. The enemy, although he may not know all the details related to their ministries, understands that God has placed a special mark on them for some purpose. Therefore, he has been hindering them since birth!

The momentary sufferings they've endured go hand in hand with the purification of their faith. Paul referred to the suffering that the righteous endure as light afflictions. This is the process that a Christian chooses to undergo when he desires to become an honorable vessel with a continual flow of the "golden" oil. Although God is not the author of adversity and the fiery trials that come to destroy our faith, the heat refines us (if we refuse to get offended), which enlarges more of our hearts for God.

The two witnesses will be able to share in the same suffering as Paul, who said,

> We were crushed and overwhelmed beyond our
> ability to endure, and we thought we would never
> live through it. (2 Cor. 1:8)

Jesus endured the same force of pressure from the kingdom of darkness. Prior to Jesus going to the cross, He went to Gethsemane, which was on the side of the Mount of Olives. Gethsemane means "the place where olive oil is pressed." At an olive press, olives were gathered into sacks and stacked on top of one another. A heavy beam was lowered to press the oil from the olives. The more pressure, the more oil.

It was here in the Garden of Gethsemane that Jesus was pressed beyond measure. He began to be deeply distressed and troubled, saying, "My soul is overwhelmed with sorrow to the point of death" (Mark 14:34).

The agony He endured before His crucifixion created such an intense pressure upon His physical body that scriptures say His sweat was like great drops of blood falling from Him (Luke 22:44).

In like manner, we must be willing to go to the Garden of Gethsemane to be pressed. The trying of our faith in Gethsemane will produce patience. This is the process required for manufacturing the oil (anointing).

In pursuit of the double portion anointing (oil), Elisha made this same journey—the journey of becoming dead to self but alive to righteousness.

In 2 Kings 2, Elisha requested a double portion of Elijah's spirit, which was a reference to the oil that emanated from his mentor for the purpose of miracles.

> Elijah questioned Elisha, "Tell me, what can I do for you before I am taken from you?" Elisha replied, "Let me inherit a double portion of your spirit." Elijah answered, saying, "You have asked a difficult thing." (2 Kings 2:9–10)

However, Elisha made the laborious journey through Gilgal, Bethel, Jericho, and Jordan. Interestingly, the scripture records exactly twice as many miracles through Elisha (twenty-eight miracles) as took place through Elijah (fourteen miracles).

Not all double portions convey blessing, however. Revelation 18:6 speaks of judgment upon Babylon, stating, "Pay her back as she herself has paid back others, and repay her double for her deeds; mix a double portion for her in the cup she mixed."

Here, the double portion indicates a heavy judgment. The idea behind the term is still that of a *great amount*.

We must be aware that God does not mix the contents of the cup of Babylon with His own; they are totally incompatible. Paul says, "We cannot drink of the Lord's cup and of the cup of demons" (1 Cor. 10:21). We must choose one or the other.

At that time, those who are making deals with Babylon and selling their precious cargo for ill-gotten gains will not be allowed into the marriage supper of the Lamb.

The last part of the parable of the ten virgins reveals that the doors will be shut on those who waited till it was too late to get oil for the lamps.

> But while they were on their way to buy the oil, the bridegroom arrived. The virgins who were ready went in with him to the wedding banquet. And the door was shut. Later the others also came. "Lord, Lord," they said, "open the door for us!" But he replied, "Truly I tell you, I don't know you." Therefore keep watch, because you do not know the day or the hour. (Matt. 25:10–13)

There will be many who mingled with Babylon for way too long. They lived for selfish gain and thought they could be right with God if they *ran with* the wise.

The Church is often among those in the world who are most corrupt. She is anything but the virgin bride prepared to meet the Groom. She has prostituted herself out for money. Paul saw this in his day: "For we do not market the word of God for profit like so many" (2 Cor. 2:17).

At this present time, to which group do you belong: to the wise or foolish? The difference rests in whether or not you have chosen to buy the oil. By denying His Spirit, we reject the supply of oil (anointing). Without the anointing, we only have a form of godliness because we are denying His power to transform us. Do you trust His refining process?

We will not make it into "the city" off someone else's anointing. A personal journey is required. As is evident from the parable of the ten virgins, the oil cannot be borrowed. Although Babylon is currently mixed in with the Church, there will come a time when those who are defiled, *the foolish*, will not be able to steal the cup of salvation from which *the wise* partake. Proverbs 5:15 says, "Drink water from your own cistern, running water from your own well."

As the parable goes, the two categories of people are finally separated, as one group will be accepted in and the remaining populace of unprepared subjects will be left outside the doors in outer darkness.

> Outside the city are the dogs—the sorcerers, the sexually immoral, the murderers, the idol worshippers, and all who love to live a lie. (Rev. 22:15)

According to the parable, they *claimed* to know God. But He replied, "Truly I tell you, I don't know you" (Matt. 25:12).

The two witnesses will be two of the golden oil vendors who have laid down their lives for the world. The hardships they suffer will "press them" until their eventual death. However, their testimonies will continue to live on through their words and deeds, and the golden oil that decants from them will provide light for the whole world, especially the Church.

Although they will be scorned and mocked by the world, the Church should heed the words and counsels of God's two end-time prophets, lest she be a part of the foolish, unwise, and unprepared who missed the Bridegroom.

The Outer Court of the Temple

The pattern of the Old Testament tabernacle was given by God in a vision to Moses and then later constructed by the human hands of the children of Israel. According to the Bible, the tabernacle, which means "residence" or "dwelling place," *was* the portable earthly dwelling place of God. It was transported by the Israelites throughout their wilderness journey. Hundreds of years later, Solomon's temple in Jerusalem superseded it as God's *permanent* dwelling place among His people.

Each and every detail of the ancient tabernacle carries spiritual significance. The tabernacle structure symbolizes a few different things: it parallels the layout and design of heaven and is a model for the present-day temple (the human heart), which houses the presence of God's Spirit within the three dimensions (spirit, soul, and body).

Through the prophet Moses, God revealed a pattern of worship that paralleled His holiness while simultaneously allowing sinful man to enter His presence. God used the pattern of tabernacle worship to reveal all that was involved with the blood of a sacrifice and atonement, which prepared His people for the sacrifice of the Lamb of God.

The journey toward freedom began with an awareness of sin in one's life. When an Israelite recognized that sin was destroying him, he would make his way to the tabernacle (God's presence) for forgiveness.

There were three parts of the tabernacle: (1) the outer court, (2) the Holy Place, and (3) the Holy of Holies. There was a brocade curtain that separated the Holy Place from the Most Holy Place.

The outer court was where sin was dealt with. The priest would make sacrifices on behalf of the sinner who pleaded for forgiveness.

This was symbolic of the sacrifice of Jesus's shed blood when we approach Him for the forgiveness of our sins. The outer court was also a place for cleansing. The laver could be found here so that the priest could wash with water after the sacrifice. The cleansing acts in the outer court represented the believer's baptism of water, his outward profession of the purification of sins made possible through the blood of Christ.

The inner sanctuary of the tabernacle represents the inner dimensions of a man's soul (the Holy Place) and his spirit (the Most Holy Place) when he invites the Lord to dwell in his heart.

In the Old Testament tabernacle, no one except the priests or high priests could enter these areas of God's holiness. The Holy Place was the arena for priestly service throughout the year, while only the high priest could enter the Most Holy Place once a year and then on the Day of Atonement (Lev. 16).

Access was restricted to the Most Holy Place (also called the Holy of Holies) because it was the place in the tabernacle/temple where God made His presence felt most strongly (Exod. 25:22, 26:34). Since the high priest was also a sinful man, it posed a danger for him to make daily appearances in the presence of God's holiness. Men who had trampled on the holiness of God by disregarding the power of it were killed and later served as examples of why it was important to limit access to the Most Holy Place. The good news is this: when Jesus died on the cross, the veil that existed between the Holy Place and the Most Holy Place was and has been torn forevermore as we now have access (by the blood) to come boldly before the throne room to obtain mercy and find grace to help in the time of need. In addition, Jesus brought the kingdom of heaven to the temple of man's heart. We house His presence within and are now reservoirs for His power. God's ambassador for the New Testament covenant, Paul the Apostle, asked the Corinthian Church this question:

> Do you not know that you are God's temple
> and that God's Spirit dwells in you? If anyone
> destroys God's temple, God will destroy him. For

> God's temple is holy, and you are that temple. (1
> Cor. 3:16–17)

The Old Testament temple changed locations under the new covenant as it would become the temple of a man's heart. The outer court represents the body (the covering) that God has asked us to cleanse.

> But if [you are living] by the [power of the Holy]
> Spirit you are *habitually* putting to death the sin-
> ful deeds of the body, you will [really] live for-
> ever. (Rom. 8:13)

As important as it was to adhere to the cleansing rituals performed in the outer court, it was merely preparation for entering into the inner dimension—the presence of God in the Holy Place and the Holy of Holies. God never intended for us to remain in the outer court but to enter into the inner court, which represents entering into an intimate (personal) relationship with Him. God desires for us to grow deeper in faith toward Him so that we can experience the fullness of His kingdom's benefits.

The whole tabernacle was completely set apart from sin, as it was a place for worship and sacrifices to God. However, we are living in the last days, when the heathen and the infidel are refusing to clean up their lives from idolatry (the outer court of their bodies). Up to this time, those who work iniquity have been allowed to mix themselves within the sheepfold. The time is coming very soon when God will give His prophets, the two witnesses, the directive to "exclude" the wicked and unbelieving. When God says, "Leave them out," He is really saying, "Cast them out!" God gave John the Revelator a vision of these things:

> But do not measure the outer courtyard, for it
> has been turned over to the nations. They will
> trample the holy city for 42 months. (Rev. 11:2)

In a vision (Rev. 11), John the Revelator was instructed to measure the temple of God and the altar (and to count the worshippers). However, he was also instructed to *exclude* the outer court: "Do not measure it" (verse 2).

In those times, God will appoint the two witnesses, empowering them to do mighty works. Meanwhile, the outer court of the temple (along with the holy city) will be *given* to the Gentiles, which means that although it occupied the area near the inner sanctuary, those who worshipped there would not be *accepted* inside. Instead, it (the outer court) would be designated for pagans and strangers. The outer court would be occupied by the congregation of people (Gentiles) who were *outside* the true Church, those not regarded as the people of God.

The word *outer* in *outer court* is *exóthen*, which means "from without, from outside, the outside, outside of doors." John was instructed to "leave it out" and "measure it not." The words *leave out* in the margin says "cast out." These words imply more than just an omission because it comes from the word *ekballo*, which means "to throw out, cast out, put out, banish, and to leave." God will ask the Church to cast out the unbelieving and leave them to their own destruction (ruin).

It is evident from the scripture previously mentioned that God will urge His two prophets to create a barrier that will *cut off* the wicked. This will occur in a moment of conflict, strife, and hostility between God's righteous and those who oppose His building endeavors.

Resultantly, the Church will build a wall to exclude the wicked who are trampling on the sacred things of God. Perhaps these walls are metaphorical, symbolizing the barriers that we create through prayer to oppose the wicked. Or maybe this is a reference to the distance (separation) we make as we come out from among the world (Babylon) and its idolatries. However, the new city that is being developed by the Church, which eventually comes down as New Jerusalem, will have high walls and large gates. It will be an enclosed city, and only those who have washed their robes will be allowed to enter.

> And he carried me away in the Spirit to a vast and lofty mountain, and showed me the holy [sanctified] city of Jerusalem coming down out of heaven from God…it had a massive and high wall, with twelve [large] gates. The city is laid out as a square, its length being the same as its width; and he measured the city with his rod—twelve thousand stadia [about 1,400 miles]; its length and width and height are equal. He measured its wall also—a hundred forty-four cubits [about 200 feet]. The wall was built of jasper… (Rev. 21:10, 12, 16–18)

The city will be a square that has four high walls (Rev. 21:13). The walls will exclude the idolatrous and unbelieving who refuse to cleanse themselves of sin in the outer court.

> As a result, those who are left outside the city walls will themselves be trampled in the winepress of God's wrath. (Rev. 14:20)

> Outside the city are the dogs—the sorcerers, the sexually immoral, the murderers, the idol worshippers, and all who love to live a lie. (Rev. 22:15)

This concept of the wicked being *separated* and *locked out* is demonstrated in Jesus's parable of the ten virgins.

> But while they (the five foolish virgins) were going away to buy *oil*, the bridegroom came, and those who were ready went in with him to the wedding feast; and the door was shut *and* locked. Afterward came also the other virgins, saying, "Lord, Lord, open to us." But he answered,

"Truly I say to you, I do not know you." (Matt. 25:10–12)

Jesus referred to the venue where the bride (the Church) and the Bridegroom (Jesus) consummate their marriage as the bridal chamber. Generally speaking, the bridal chamber is the room in which wedding celebrations or ceremonies take place. More specifically, it may also refer to a place even more intimate—the bedroom used by a newly married couple.

> And Jesus said unto them, "Can the children of the bridal chamber mourn, as long as the bridegroom is with them? But the days will come, when the bridegroom shall be taken from them, and then shall they fast." (Matt. 9:15)

The inner sanctuary of the Old Testament tabernacle was a model for the *intimate bridal chamber* in the parable just mentioned. It represents the wedding hall where the marriage supper of the Lamb will take place upon the return of the Groom. We are God's *children of the bridal chamber* (by kinship) and the *bride of Christ.*

In another parable, Jesus proved that the inner sanctuary measured in Revelation 21 will be a wedding hall filled with innumerable guests. He taught, saying,

> The kingdom of heaven may be compared to a king who gave a wedding feast for his son, and sent his servants to call those who were invited to the wedding feast, but they would not come. Again he sent other servants, saying, "Tell those who are invited, 'See, I have prepared my dinner, my oxen and my fat calves have been slaughtered, and everything is ready. Come to the wedding feast.'" But they paid no attention and went off, one to his farm, another to his business, while the rest seized his servants, treated them shamefully,

and killed them. The king was angry, and he sent his troops and destroyed those murderers and burned their city. Then he said to his servants, "The wedding feast is ready, but those invited were not worthy. Go therefore to the main roads and invite to the wedding feast as many as you find." And those servants went out into the roads and gathered all whom they found, both bad and good. So the wedding hall was filled with guests. But when the king came in to look at the guests, he saw there a man who had no wedding garment. And he said to him, "Friend, how did you get in here without a wedding garment?" And he was speechless. Then the king said to the attendants, "Bind him hand and foot and cast him into the outer darkness. In that place there will be weeping and gnashing of teeth." For many are called, but few are chosen. (Matt. 22:1–14)

The wedding hall is being prepared to be filled with innumerable guests. God's servants are sending out invitations and bidding all to come.

Also worthy of special attention is the guest in Jesus's parable who was not properly dressed for the wedding banquet. As the story indicates, he was *cast out* by the King. Where was he cast then? From this parable, Jesus taught that he was cast into outer darkness. The word *outer* in *outer darkness* is *exóteros*, which means "outmost, external, exterior, outside, and without." According to the *Strong's Concordance*, this was a place *outside* the limits of the lit palace (to which the Messiah's kingdom is here likened). The exclusion of the wicked, the tares, is a sure sign that the bride of Christ is growing weary of waiting on the Groom. This is the Church's way of getting cleaned up (washing her robes) and getting adorned for her union with Christ.

The words "But do not measure the outer courtyard" are resounding in the spirit realm: "For it has been turned over to the nations" (Rev. 11:2). The work of excluding the outer court will begin through the ministries of God's two end-time prophets.

Not only will the outer court be given to the wicked but they will also seize the holy city, trampling on it for three and a half years. Three and a half years is the exact duration of the witnesses' prophetic ministries on earth. The three and a half years are significant because it marks the middle of the seven-year peace agreement. The prophet Daniel wrote about this centuries ago, saying,

> That ruler will have a firm agreement with many people for seven years, and when half this time is past [three and a half years], he will put an end to sacrifices and offerings. The Awful Horror will be placed on the highest point of the Temple and will remain there until the one who put it there meets the end which God has prepared for him. (Dan. 9:27)

Somewhere in the middle of the seven-year peace agreement, "when half this time is past," the Antichrist will put an end to various Christian practices and will commit ungodly acts to desecrate the temple and the holy things of God. Second Thessalonians 2:4 says that he will oppose and exalt himself so proudly and so insolently above every so-called god or object of worship so that he actually enters and takes his seat in the temple of God, publicly proclaiming that he himself is God. The saints and the holy place will actually be under subjection to him for three and a half years. He will "trample" on them and the holy city. Daniel 7:25 says,

> He [the Antichrist] will speak words against the Most High [God] and wear down the saints of the Most High, and he will intend to change the times and the law; and they will be given into his hand for a time, [two] times, and half a time [three and one-half years].

From this verse, it is safe to infer that the Church will still be on earth at this time since the Antichrist will "wear down the saints" and "be given into his hand for three and a half years." Like Zerubbabel and Joshua, who were given sanction to rebuild the temple in Jerusalem (Zech. 4:9), the two witnesses will aid in building the temple (assumingly metaphorical) in the last days. As they prophesy, God will naturally begin to sift and separate the wheat from the tares. People will make their choices of whom they'll obey and serve. The outer court will be cut off, as it will now be deemed *outside* the presence of God.

At this time, it is imperative for men to withdraw themselves from Babylon for two main reasons: (1) so that they are not locked outside the city doors and (2) to escape her (Babylon's) plagues (judgment).

> Then I heard another voice calling from heaven, "Come away from her [Babylon], my people. Do not take part in her sins, or you will be punished with her." (Rev. 18:4)

The separation is necessary as the angels begin to harvest the earth. God's harvest represents those who have washed their robes in the blood of Christ.

> Then I saw a white cloud, and seated on the cloud was someone like the Son of Man. He had a gold crown on his head and a sharp sickle in his hand. Then another angel came from the Temple and shouted to the one sitting on the cloud, "Swing the sickle, for the time of harvest has come; the crop on earth is ripe." So the one sitting on the cloud swung his sickle over the earth, and the whole earth was harvested. After that, another angel came from the Temple in heaven, and he also had a sharp sickle. Then another angel, who had power to destroy with fire, came from the

> altar. He shouted to the angel with the sharp sickle, "Swing your sickle now to gather the clusters of grapes from the vines of the earth, for they are ripe for judgment." So the angel swung his sickle over the earth and loaded the grapes into the great winepress of God's wrath. The grapes were trampled in the winepress outside the city, and blood flowed from the winepress in a stream about 180 miles long and as high as a horse's bridle. (Rev. 14:14–20)

After the Church is raptured out, many will be left behind. Verse 20 indicates that the wicked will be *trampled*, which insinuates the Church's position of authority (above them). No longer will the heathen be allowed to trample on God's righteous and the holy city. The angel who has the power to destroy with fire will proceed from the altar, administering justice. God's fiery judgment will befall those who are excluded (left out). Notice the words in the verse aforementioned: "they were trampled in the winepress of God's wrath *outside the city.*"

The ministries of the two witnesses will be accompanied by clarity and revelation that generates movement within the Church. The movement will transition into a momentum that causes the members of Christ's body to stand erect. She will assertively begin to remove the stumbling blocks that wreak havoc on the Church assembly.

It is time to build a wall that will exclude the sorcerers. We are living in a time when God is instructing us to "leave them out." Henceforth, they will be *cast out* into what is known as outer darkness, a temporary suffering that is expiatory and purifying, not punitive like hellfire. In turn, the wheat will be gathered and brought into the barn. The separation of the wheat and the tares proves that the body of Christ has come out from among Babylon and washed her robes in preparation for the wedding banquet. The two witnesses will testify of these things and give approval of the marriage. Then they will lay down their lives and be caught up with God in heaven before many witnesses.

The Two Olive Trees

> These two prophets are the two olive trees and
> the two lampstands that stand before the Lord of
> all the earth. (Rev. 11:4)

In the book of Revelation, the two witnesses are referred to as olive trees. In the Old Testament book of Zechariah, the prophet described them as olive trees *and* olive branches:

> Then I said to him, "What are these two olive
> trees on the right and the left of the lampstand?"
> And a second time I answered and said to him,
> "What are these two branches of the olive trees,
> which are beside the two golden pipes from which
> the golden oil is poured out?" (Zech. 4:11–14)

Why would these end-time prophets, individuals who house such great power to testify, prophesy, and administer justice, be likened to olive trees? What is the significance of the *tree* as a symbol for these two oracles of God?

In the beginning, there were two trees in the garden whose kingdoms opposed one another. Although the tree of life was in the very center of the Garden of Eden, also present was the tree of the knowledge of good and evil. As a matter of fact, it was placed right beside the tree of life.

> In the middle of the garden were the tree of life
> and the tree of the knowledge of good and evil.
> (Gen. 2:9)

I find it interesting that there were two paths laid out for man, even when he was in a state of immortality.

The book of Enoch is insightful, giving us a more in-depth look at these things in Genesis. Enoch wrote explicitly of these two trees in his writing. His writings provide additional commentary on the topic of the two trees, which will give us a better perspective for the study.

Imagine that. One of the first men mentioned in Bible history, Enoch, gave vivid descriptions of both trees centuries before the Bible was ever compiled. Of the evil tree, he says,

> And I came to the Garden of Righteousness, and saw beyond those trees many large trees growing there and of goodly fragrance, large, very beautiful and glorious, and the tree of wisdom whereof they eat and know great wisdom. That tree is in height like the fir, and its leaves are like [those of] the Carob tree: and its fruit is like the clusters of the vine, very beautiful: and the fragrance of the tree penetrates afar. Then I said: "How beautiful is the tree, and how attractive is its look!" Then Raphael the holy angel, who was with me, answered me and said: "This is the tree of wisdom, of which thy father old [in years] and thy aged mother, who were before thee, have eaten, and they learnt wisdom and their eyes were opened, and they knew that they were naked and they were driven out of the garden." (Enoch 32:3–6)

Here, Enoch describes the alluring fragrance of the satanic tree, revealing its great enticing appeal. He was swept away by its beauty and fragrance, which had the ability to "penetrate from afar." Indeed, it was a sight to behold. The holy angel revealed to him that this was the tree of wisdom that raised such curiosity it caused Adam and Eve to forfeit everything for its fruit (promises). Enoch was enamored by the splendor of this evil tree. He said, "How beautiful the tree is, and how attractive it looks!" This tree is representative of Satan, whose beauty he possessed (as an anointed cherub) was something to behold.

In Ezekiel 28:12, God spoke of Lucifer's beauty before the fall: "You were the seal of perfection, full of wisdom and perfect in beauty."

Notice how he was described as "full of wisdom and perfect in beauty." This is the very same description given for the evil tree in the book of Enoch.

In Ezekiel 28, he was described as being "full of wisdom and perfect in beauty," and in Enoch 32, the angel of God called this amazingly beautiful tree the *tree of wisdom.*

In contrast to the twisted tree was the tree of life. Enoch recorded details concerning it in chapters 24 and 25:

> And from thence I went to another place of the earth, and he showed me...fragrant trees that encircled the throne. And amongst them was a tree such as I had never yet smelt, neither was any amongst them nor were others like it: it had a fragrance beyond all fragrance, and its leaves and blooms and wood wither not for ever: and its fruit is beautiful, and its fruit resembles the dates of a palm. Then I said: beautiful is this tree, and fragrant, and its leaves are fair, and its blooms delightful in appearance. Then answered Michael, one of the holy and honoured angels who was with me, and was their leader. And he said unto me: "Enoch, why dost thou ask me regarding the fragrance of the tree, and dost thou wish to learn the truth?" Then I answered him:

"I wish to know about everything, but especially about this tree." And he answered saying… And as for this fragrant tree no mortal is permitted to touch it till the great judgment, when He shall take vengeance on all and bring [everything] to its consummation for ever. It shall then be given to the righteous and holy. Its fruit shall be for food to the elect: it shall be transplanted to the holy place, to the temple of the Lord, the Eternal King. Then shall they rejoice with joy and be glad, And into the holy place shall they enter; And its fragrance shall be in their bones, And they shall live a long life on earth, Such as thy fathers lived: And in their days shall no plague Or torment or calamity touch them. Then blessed I the God of Glory, the Eternal King, who hath prepared such things for the righteous, and hath created them and promised to give to them.

Overcome with curiosity, Enoch was exceedingly desirous to obtain knowledge of the tree of life and said, "I wish to know about everything, but especially about this tree."

This brings us great insight into the tree of life. Not only is the tree of life beautiful to behold but Enoch was also captivated by its fragrance. He said, "And amongst them was a tree such as I had never yet smelt, neither was any amongst them nor were others like it: it had a fragrance beyond all fragrance."

The apostle Paul was well-acquainted with the fragrance of this same tree. Writing to the Corinthians, he said,

But thanks be to God, who always leads us trium-phantly in Christ and through us spreads every-where the fragrance of the knowledge of Him. For we are to God the sweet aroma of Christ… (2 Cor. 2:14–15)

Notice the phrase "through us spreads everywhere the fragrance of knowledge." In other words, having a revealed knowledge of God will emit a beautiful aroma that will spread everywhere. As a result, the knowledge of the glory of God will cover the earth according to scripture. The gospel will be published throughout the earth via the fragrance (emissions) of the members of Christ's body.

> For the earth will be filled with the knowledge of
> the glory of the LORD, as the waters cover the sea.
> (Hab. 2:14)

This information mirrors that recorded by Enoch thousands of years prior to the apostle Paul. As did Enoch, Paul clearly understood that both the tree of life and Jesus were synonymous with each other. Notice the main characteristic of the tree of life: it gives life. Moreover, didn't Jesus come to give the same life? He said in John 10:10, "The thief comes only to steal and kill and destroy. I came that they may have life and have it abundantly."

If we house the presence of Christ, the same sweet fragrance emanates from us that came from the tree of life. The same healing power that came from the leaves of the tree of life flows through us (Rev. 22:2). The tree symbolizes Jesus and the good news that is published by the members of Christ's body throughout the earth "are to God the sweet aroma of Christ" (2 Cor. 2:15).

Through the Acts of the Apostles and epistles, God used Paul as His ambassador to reach out to the Gentile (non-Jewish) people. Paul associated this union with a branch from a "wild" olive tree that had been grafted into the rich nourishment of God's "special" olive tree (the tree of life):

> But some of these branches from Abraham's
> tree—some of the people of Israel—have been
> broken off. And you Gentiles, who were branches
> from a wild olive tree, have been grafted in. So
> now you also receive the blessing God has prom-
> ised Abraham and his children, sharing in the

rich nourishment from the root of God's special
olive tree. (Rom. 11:17)

The Church body has become "the branches" that have been grafted into the rich nourishment of the olive tree, God's tree of life. Hence, this was God's intention for His people in the garden of paradise, even from the beginning of time. In Revelations 21 and 22, John describes the vision of the restoration of Eden. God gave him a vision of the holy city, the New Jerusalem, coming down from heaven in its perfect state, as in the beginning.

It goes back to the beginning, with the two trees that stood beside each other in the center of the garden. As an individual, our hearts decide which tree we wish to become an extension of. Jesus gives substance to the truth of this concept:

I am the vine; you are the branches. If you remain
in me and I in you, you will bear much fruit;
apart from me you can do nothing. (John 15:5)

Therefore, we are individually a branch of one of the two types of trees.

By the same token, the two witnesses will be on the earth as branches of the olive tree, emanating the sweet aroma of Christ for the duration of their three-and-a-half-year ministries. As the sweetest of perfumes, the aroma of the good news from their testimonies will extend throughout the world, reaching across the globe to all seven continents. Men, women, boys, and girls will be penetrated to the bone by the sweet fragrance of Christ's offering. However, the same fragrance that emanates from God's chosen oracles will be a stench in the nostrils of the ungodly:

But thank God! He has made us his captives and
continues to lead us along in Christ's triumphal
procession. Now he uses us to spread the knowledge of Christ everywhere, like a sweet perfume.
Our lives are a Christ-like fragrance rising up to

> God. But this fragrance is perceived differently
> by those who are being saved and by those who
> are perishing. To those who are perishing, we are
> a dreadful smell of death and doom. But to those
> who are being saved, we are a life-giving perfume.
> And who is adequate for such a task as this? (2
> Cor. 2:14–16)

Indeed, by the end of their three-and-a-half-year testimonies, there will be a marked distinction between the wheat and the tares. The consuming fire released from their mouths will create a perfect chasm for the harvesting angels. False prophets and deceivers will be naked and exposed to the gaze of all. The stumbling blocks will be cast away, creating a clear path for the righteous. Some will be drawn to the compelling grace of the two witnesses; others will be appalled by their words and deeds to the extent that they applaud at the sight of their dead bodies lying in the streets. These are the two olive trees of Revelation 11 that stand before the Lord of the earth.

All throughout the Bible, in both the Old and New Testaments, the tree is used as a symbol for spiritual "kingdoms." The two trees in the center of the Garden of Eden represented two "opposing kingdoms." The first, of God's light (and life); the other, of satanic darkness (and death). As a matter of fact, Jesus likened "God's kingdom" to a tree, even in the New Testament.

> Again he said, "What shall we say the kingdom
> of God is like, or what parable shall we use to
> describe it? It is like a mustard seed, which is the
> smallest of all seeds on earth. Yet when planted,
> it grows and becomes the largest of all garden
> plants, with such big branches that the birds can
> perch in its shade." (Mark 4:30–32)

Jesus asked the question, "What can I most accurately compare God's kingdom with?" And then He answered his own question with

"God's kingdom most resembles a tree where the nations of the earth may inhabit."

Here, Jesus compared God's kingdom to a tree that began as a seedling, whose branches eventually spanned to produce shade and lodging for all who gather under its shadowing canopy. As a matter of fact, Genesis 2 says that God planted it Himself.

Apparently, both trees were not just placed but "planted" (as seed) into the soil bed of the garden because Genesis 2:8 says, "The Lord God 'planted' a garden in Eden." The succeeding verse reveals that God made every tree to spring forth "out of the ground" that was pleasant to the sight and good for food (verse 9). These two verses confirm that both the tree of life and the tree of the knowledge of good and evil that were in the middle of the garden grew from a planted seed. However, the two trees were from two different "types" of seed. The tree of life came from the seed of God, while the tree of the knowledge of good and evil was contaminated, becoming the seed of Satan.

The tree of life was the "good tree" that God had spoken of beforehand through the Old Testament prophet Ezekiel, saying,

> On the mountain heights of Israel I will plant it; it will produce branches and bear fruit and become a splendid cedar. Birds of every kind will nest in it; they will find shelter in the shade of its branches. All the trees of the forest will know that I the Lord bring down the tall tree and make the low tree grow tall. I dry up the green tree and make the dry tree flourish. I the Lord have spoken, and I will do it. (Ezek. 17:23–24)

What a refreshing promise for God's inhabitants to be under the shadow (branches) of the Almighty. Notice in the verses aforementioned, however, that there are two opposing trees mentioned. As this same prophecy unfolds in Ezekiel 17, God speaks concerning the judgment of the wicked tree, more specifically, the "kingdom" that opposes God's righteous people.

Say to them, "This is what the Sovereign Lord
says: Will it thrive? Will it not be uprooted and
stripped of its fruit so that it withers? All its new
growth will wither. It will not take a strong arm
or many people to pull it up by the roots. It has
been planted, but will it thrive? Will it not wither
completely when the east wind strikes it-wither
away in the plot where it grew?" (Verses 9–10)

In November 2019, the Lord gave me a dream in the early morning. I was impacted by the details of the dream and found myself rehearsing it many times over in my mind. In the dream, I was standing beside a country shed in an open field just after sundown. Although I can't recall who was inside the shed, it seems they might have been praying for me. Facing the eastern sky, I observed a few separate funnel clouds forming. I remember thinking that I hoped the storm didn't turn in my direction. One of the funnel clouds, however, blew toward me, but I only felt the very border of its slight wind. I recall praying within myself for God to protect me. In a moment, God Himself pulled all the funnel clouds together as if He bound them together into one with His outstretched arms. He moved them away from me, to a distant place farther east. It was then that I heard an authoritative voice ring out from heaven. The words, however, were incomprehensible. Yet what I do know is that at its command, things in both heaven and earth moved immediately. The skies were filled with the awe and wonder of God; a reverential fear took possession of the atmosphere. The funnel clouds that God had bound into one place transformed into burning hot volcanic lava that was thrown down to the earth forcefully. When the hot lava struck the earth, I cringed at the thought of what or who it might have destroyed, because there was no escape from it. However, God had forced the fiery molten lava into a tree without doing harm to any persons, properties, or animals. I recall having thought how good the grace of God was, to force these destructive winds into one place and into a single tree, to keep them from harming His living creation and their things. As I peered into the eastern sky from a distance,

I observed how the fire so swiftly consumed every part of the tree. Even from so far away, I could hear the branches popping and crackling from the hostile fires that wasted it. What was God trying to convey to me from this dream that teemed with spiritual symbolism? I refused to jump to conclusions about the mystery of the burning tree. Instead, I prayed for the correct interpretation.

Since then, God has shown me that the tree in the prophecy of Ezekiel 17, which will eventually come under final judgment, is the same wicked tree that was set ablaze in my dream. When the time is right, God's consuming fires will ravage Satan's kingdom in a single hour. Scriptures indicate that this wicked tree is an emblem of the "kingdom Babylon," Satan's witchcraft kingdom, the culmination of all moral and spiritual depravity. This tree is continuously competing for height and stature over God's kingdom. Kingdom Babylon is an extension of the evil tree of the knowledge of good and evil that stood in the midst of the Garden of Eden, from which the serpent beguiled the first of God's created man and woman. This tree is mentioned all throughout the Old and New Testament scriptures, but it is likely that we have failed to understand its significance. However, we may notice it being repeated in Babylonian history.

In ancient history, Nebuchadnezzar was the king of wicked Babylon. In the midst of Babylon's height, prosperity, and splendor, God gave Nebuchadnezzar a dream of a tree. The story is found in the book of Daniel 4. The tree in Nebuchadnezzar's dream was enormous in stature, but God would cut it down to the size of a stump without uprooting it. The words of king Nebuchadnezzar were these:

> These were the visions of my head while on my bed: I was looking, and behold, A tree in the midst of the earth, And its height was great. The tree grew large and strong and its top touched the sky; it was visible to the ends of the earth. Its leaves were beautiful, its fruit abundant, and on it was food for all. Under it the wild animals found shelter, and the birds lived in its branches; from it every creature was fed. (Dan. 4:10–12)

The interpretation of Nebuchadnezzar's dream came through God's prophet Daniel and is recorded in the same chapter. He explained to King Nebuchadnezzar, saying,

> The tree you saw, which grew large and strong, with its top touching the sky, visible to the whole earth, with beautiful leaves and abundant fruit, providing food for all, giving shelter to the wild animals, and having nesting places in its branches for the birds, Your Majesty, you are that tree! You have become great and strong; your greatness has grown until it reaches the sky, and your dominion extends to distant parts of the earth. (Dan. 4:20–22)

You see, Nebuchadnezzar had become an extension of the wrong tree, "kingdom Babylon." God revealed to him through a dream that he was part of a kingdom that was going to be judged by God and cut down to a stump. As a matter of fact, Nebuchadnezzar was one of its very own branches.

Jesus, on the other hand, was the seed that fell to the ground and died (John 12:24). He was the branch from the stump of Jesse (Isa. 11:1) that will blossom and reveal the glory of God's kingdom in all its brilliance and glorious splendor. Isaiah prophesied about this king (Jesus) and foretold of His coming:

> The royal line of David is like a tree that has been cut down; but just as new branches sprout from a stump, so a new king will arise from among David's descendants (Isa. 11:1)

The aforementioned dream recorded in Daniel 4, however, revealed that Nebuchadnezzar was engrafted into Satan's tree, the Babylonian kingdom.

Through an angelic messenger, God announces the final destruction of the kingdom of Babylon, which sprung out from this tree of death.

> With a mighty voice he shouted: "Fallen! Fallen is Babylon the Great! She has become a dwelling for demons and a haunt for every impure spirit, a haunt for every unclean bird, a haunt for every unclean and detestable animal." (Rev. 18:2)

Verses 8–10 go on to say,

> In one day her plagues will overtake her: death, mourning and famine. She will be consumed by fire, for mighty is the Lord God who judges her. When the kings of the earth who committed adultery with her and shared her luxury see the smoke of her burning, they will weep and mourn over her. Terrified at her torment, they will stand far off and cry: "Woe! Woe to you, great city, you mighty city of Babylon! In one hour your doom has come!"

Notice the words in verse 8, "She will be consumed by fire." These words parallel the dream God gave me of the burning tree. The words of John's prophecy in Revelation are alive and remain. Kingdom Babylon is soon to be judged. All those who have lodged in her branches will be scattered as an act of God's mercy. We will all peer from a distance to witness her destruction. The fire of God will consume her in one hour. As Revelation 18:7 says, "Her own plagues will overtake her." God will cause the destructive winds that she releases to turn back on her, just as I saw it happen in my dream. He will issue His decree from the heavens and consume her with His fire.

It is then at the appointed time that God will heal the nations and the wounds of all people. His own kingdom (the tree of life) will begin to sprout, blossom, and flourish. This will give rise to the meaning of Revelation 22:2:

> On each side of the river stood the tree of life,
> bearing twelve crops of fruit, yielding its fruit
> every month. And the leaves of the tree are for
> the healing of the nations.

The word *healing*, "healing of the nations," is *therapeia*, where we get our word *therapy*. It's defined as "care, attention, especially medical attention [treatment], those who render service."

The existence of soul wounds is extremely prevalent among people today, but very few seem to have the knowledge to prepare a dressing and bind up the wound of their neighbor. I'm reminded of the story Jesus told about the Good Samaritan. The parable says that the Good Samaritan made a dressing for the injury of the traveler. He bound up the man's wounds and poured in the oil and the wine. What does the oil and the wine represent? The answer can be found in Psalm 104:15:

> You make wine to cheer human hearts, olive oil
> to make faces shine, and bread to strengthen
> human hearts.

The oil represents the anointing that destroys the yokes. When the anointing does its work, the soul will be free from pain and the face will shine. When people feel the freedom of being liberated, they will smile again. According to Isaiah 1:6, olive oil was used as a soothing ointment for infected wounds.

> From the sole of your foot to the top of your
> head there is no soundness—only wounds and
> welts and open sores, not cleansed or bandaged
> or soothed with olive oil (Isa. 1:6)

The wine and oil are two ingredients used for the healing recipe to treat the infected wound of the fallen man in this story. In the book of Jeremiah, we read where God was asking about a healing salve that was necessary to soothe the infected wounds of His people:

> Is there no balm in Gilead? Is there no physi-
> cian there? Why then is there no healing for the
> wound of my people? (Jer. 8:22)

I believe that the medicinal application the Good Samaritan used to treat the wound of the fallen man is synonymous with the "healing balm of Gilead." God mourns when His people are crushed, and that is why He has offered us a cure, Jesus Christ, who makes men whole. When Jesus walked the earth, scriptures indicate He went about doing good and healing all who were oppressed by the devil. He made the heavy-hearted happy by healing their soul wounds, and He set free the captive, giving them a reason to smile again.

God desires to heal His people. In the end, it will be the leaves of the trees that will provide healing for the nations (Rev. 22:2)

Naturally speaking, there are many trees that exude an appealing scent. Odoriferous leaves, bark, and even roots are often rich in terpenes and terpenoids (aromatic compounds). The terpenes and terpenoids produced by conifers have anti-inflammatory, antioxidant, analgesic, and even antitumor properties, according to recent studies. Obviously, there's more to the forest's restorative benefits than the calming serenity of nature. There is even a practice in some countries called forest bathing, where people are encouraged to breathe while taking soothing meditative walks in the forest.

The two witnesses in the end will be anointed with a ministry of reconciliation. They will be like the Good Samaritan who bound the wounds of the fallen. As a result, men will be delivered and will recover from their soul wounds. These two anointed ones will pour in the oil and the wine, the kind that restores the soul. In turn, the Church will have faces that shine. The body of Christ will radiate such brilliance and sunlight that the tree of life will begin to develop its leaves and bud. As a result of the unveiling of God's Word through the prophets, the sweet fragrance will fill the entire land and the nations will be healed.

> These two prophets are the two olive trees…that
> stand before the Lord of all the earth. (Rev. 11:4)

Cutting Off the Horseleech

The exclusion of the outer court in these last days is imperative, as God is requiring Satan's evil workers of iniquity to be cut off from the land. The two witnesses will be present on the earth to lead the movement in teaching the Church *how to* build the walls of God's city so high and wide that a distinct separation occurs between the righteous and those who work iniquity. Although they will still yearn to lay hold of the life of God from the righteous, the wicked will no longer have access to the supply after the chasm has been created. They will be shut outside the city gates in what is spiritually called outer darkness, a place of momentary suffering. Outer darkness is a spiritual condition described as God's blazing furnace for those who have been excluded. It is a place of mourning for the embittered and the regretful and is accompanied by weeping and gnashing of teeth.

> So it will be at the end of the age. The angels will come forth, *separate* the wicked from among the just, and throw them into the fiery furnace, where there will be weeping and gnashing of teeth. (Matt. 13:49–50)

We as believers mustn't grant pity for those who are fighting to hang onto us for our oil (life supply). Jesus taught a parable of ten virgins. Five of the virgins were considered wise because they came prepared for the darkness of the night by bringing extra oil for their lamps. The other five were considered foolish for not bringing extra oil. When the bridegroom called (representative of Jesus coming back), the lamps of the five foolish virgins began to sputter because of a shortage of oil. These five turned to those who had oil and asked to "freely take" from theirs. The wise virgins said, "No. Go and buy your own oil from those who sell it." In other words, there is a price that one has to pay for the oil, but the "horseleeches" were trying to borrow it, crying out, "Give us your oil!" We can't just borrow our neighbor's relationship with God, their life flow, or their knowledge of Him. We need to personally possess both the lamp and the oil. Scriptures say "buy the truth," not "borrow the truth." By not having their own oil, the foolish missed the wedding feast.

Consequently, we must cut the cord from the subjects who drain us! God has given every person the choice to buy the oil for themselves, so it's high time that we part ways with these wolves in sheep's clothing. There are countless numbers of people in hell today because men enabled them and wouldn't cut them off their life supply. As a result, they never came face-to-face with the truth that can only be experienced in the furnace of outer darkness. Outer darkness is a merciful judgment, although it's only a temporary grace period, so it is time we let go of our idols and let God be the Lord of our life.

Believe it or not, God has given us great insight into spiritual demonic attachments and esoteric knowledge concerning *spiritual vampires* (leeches), who even exist in human form. Proverbs 30:15–16 says,

> The leech has two daughters: Give and Give.
> There are three things that will not be satisfied,
> Four that will not say, "Enough": the grave, the
> barren womb, the thirsty desert, the blazing fire.

Here, the word *horseleech* is *aluqah*, which is an Aramaic loanword defined as a "vampire-like demon" according to the *Strong's Concordance*.

The parasitic leech is hereby chosen as the emblem of a predator having an insatiable appetite. An insatiable creature it is, which sucks blood till it's ready to burst. In the latter portion of this verse, the "things" that are "never satisfied" and "never say enough" resemble the horseleech in its insatiableness. Perhaps we've been associated with certain people who possess these same qualities. Notice that the horseleech is crying out, "Give, give." In other words, this predator is never filled but always longing and ready to receive more and more from whomever they find life to draw from.

As the Church begins to exclude the wicked, by removing her enablers, these self-centered bloodsuckers will wither in the fire. Scriptures in Isaiah indicate that God destroys Satan's root (offspring) with "famine" (Isa. 14:30). Without a body to draw from, then, the horseleech goes hungry. For this reason, God requires isolation from workers of iniquity in these last days we live in.

The spirit of a vampire (horseleech) will indeed drain the life right out of a person unawares. It has two daughters, not just one; therefore, it wreaks double the trouble. Whereas most people have one mouth to eat from, a person with the leech spirit has two mouths, proving that it can *drain* a victim faster than he can *fill up*.

Believers shouldn't be deceived into believing they can maintain a teeming life supply while allowing a leech to feed from the life of God in them. Those who manifest the characteristics of this spirit have two mouths to the believer's one. What is scary is the fact that they're *never satisfied*. This verse attests to the truth that they have never said, "All right, I've had enough." We as believers must cut the cord (wherever the attachment has formed), lest they drain our life supply.

A horseleech, then, is *not* a giver. Do you know a person who fits this description, who has the nature of a leech? The Bible has a lot to say concerning these types of extracting predators that prey on the souls of the living. Since a horseleech is a taker, it's a perfect emblem for representing this particular class of people. If we are not careful, we ourselves as believers could fall prey to a spiritual horseleech. Scriptures indicate that they hunt for precious life. A host doesn't choose lifeless prey. They hunt for *precious* life. Without a union, a connection, or a lifeline to draw from, they are lifeless hosts.

A horseleech is a bloodsucker similar to a vampire. The blood of the body is the life of it. A leech will attach itself to a host and pull the very life from the living creature, breaking down its immunities. In essence, a horseleech has the same characteristics as a vampire in that his search for energy (food) is limited to the life of another living being. And for such reasons, God has commanded a separation from these thieves.

Let's look more deeply into the Word of God to find out what it says about these predators.

In Luke 15, we read the story of the prodigal son who had abandoned the path of wisdom and righteousness to begin a personal search for a "better life" in the world. After squandering his inheritance with riotous living, he eventually found himself in a low place, more specifically, in a pigpen. Something interesting to note: it wasn't until his enablers were removed that he turned his face toward his father's house.

This wayward son exhibits many characteristics that resemble the horseleech. One, he was in the pigpen *crying out* for food. Scriptures indicate that he would have gladly filled his stomach with the pods that the pigs ate, but *no man would give to him*. There is a key here: We must not enable others in their "hogpen" experiences. It is imperative that we *cut off* the lifeline from the leech. The medical term is "cutting the cord" in reference to the umbilical cord. The baby would never grow on its own if it remained connected to the mother after it was born. In the same way, the prodigal son would never have grown up and turned his eyes toward home if his enablers had continued to feed him the slop that the pigs ate from the troughs. Scriptures indicate that when no man would give to him, he *came to himself* (Luke 15:17). Those who had enabled the rebellious lad finally "cut the cord."

The prodigal son had a nature that was similar to the daughters of the horseleech, crying, "Give to me!" Have you ever been in the presence of someone who leaves you feeling drained and depleted of emotional, spiritual, and even physical energy? Perhaps you've had suspicions about someone in your past but reasoned it away as your own personal battle with oppression or depression. The truth is, a human vampire has probably wrapped their tentacles around you, and the energy-draining demon within them has attached itself to your spirit, soul, and body by an unseen spiritual tube/cord.

Vampires must "make a link" between themselves and a host, as it is through a link that a vampire feeds. Again, the best analogy is an unborn baby drawing life from the mother's umbilical cord. The fetus draws out life for itself from another source, through the cord. The same concept exists in the case of human vampires.

Scriptures indicate that these people *hunt souls* (Ezek. 13:18), searching for precious life (Prov. 6:26). Why? For a fact, those who hunt down and capture their hosts are not origins of a life source themselves. Perhaps they need spiritual deliverance from the sapping spirit within them that extracts the golden oil from those who supply it. Whatever the case may be, it's glaringly obvious that they do not have a healthy life source emerging from themselves and are thereby out to *steal* precious life from an external source. Notice the following scripture found in Proverbs: "Stolen water is sweet; food eaten in secret is delicious!" (Prov. 9:17).

Undoubtedly, this is the voice of a vampire spirit. It is the horseleech who cries out for *others* to give to it! It says, "Stolen water is sweet." In essence, this spirit is saying, "Don't make an investment. Just take from others. Water is sweeter when you steal it. You don't have to sow for yourself. You don't have to search for peace yourself. You don't have to find joy for yourself. Ignore God's kingdom principles of sowing and reaping for yourself and just steal it. Why plant it for yourself when you can find it in others? It's too laborious anyway."

These self-centered predators are slothful, and their inadequate life supply is so depleted that they feel forced to tap into someone else's fountain. The transference of life gives the spiritual vampire an exhilarating rush of emotions. The victim, on the other hand, may begin to feel mentally, physically, socially, emotionally, and spiritually exhausted. Over an extended period of time, a barrage of these kinds of attacks can cause breakdowns in the victim's physical body, even causing disease and physical illness. That is why it's very important to have the gift of discernment, which is the Holy Spirit's radar concerning evil spirits (attachments).

However, this is what the Lord says to the witches and warlocks who have the characteristics of a self-seeking vampire spirit:

> I am against the magic charms with which you ensnare souls like birds, and I will tear them from your arms. I will free the souls you have ensnared. I will also tear off your veils and deliver My people from your hands, so that they will no longer be prey in your hands. Then you will know that I am the LORD. (Ezek. 13:20–21)

Notice the words of the Creator: "They [my people] will no longer be prey." What an awesome promise of deliverance to those who have fallen victim to this freeloading vampire spirit.

Although there are many different methods, the vampire can feed off words (dialogue), human contact (hugs, handshakes, sex), social media, pornography, music, books, movies, TV, etc.

People who are demonized by the "vampire-like" demonic spirit often manipulate energy from their host over long distances, since this feeding method is less detectable, perhaps even at night. When links are formed and a lifeline has been established between two people, a host can use their cords as an energy-piercing gateway to the astral world for unconscious feeding. This is often carried out through dream invasion, where the energy vampire (spirit) projects into people's dreams in order to manipulate them. These types of experiences can rob a victim's rest as they wake up feeling drained and have low energy levels throughout the day.

This is actually very common, and the Bible warns us of this evil, life-extracting spirit that manifests through human instruments and workers of iniquity. This spirit operates through people who are demonized with occult powers, influence, and inclinations, whether they have a realization of this fact or not.

These demonic entities who manifest themselves through human portals are not necessarily like the vampires that we see in the movies that drain the blood. More commonly, spiritual vampires are consumers of someone else's energy and could even be drawing from your spiritual life on a daily basis if you have regular contact with someone of this nature. Most people are completely unaware of the fact that these vampire-like attacks are very real, and although they are spiritual in nature, the body and soul can also be affected. As a result, the believer's cistern (reservoir) will be left depleted of life and energy until the deep, revelatory light unveils the truth behind the wicked one. At this moment, it is imperative that the cord be cut, creating a separation from the human parasite.

Spiritual vampires come in all shapes and sizes. They are male and female, young and old, wealthy and poor. They can even be members of your own family, perhaps even your spouse.

There are distinctive traits of an energy vampire, and we must exercise our spiritual senses to discern the presence of the entities within the people with whom we have contact. As we begin to pay closer attention, we will be able to identify those who are tapping into our precious life source and leaving us drained in every capacity.

Oftentimes, the energy vampire has a spirit of rejection deeply rooted within them that can be traced back to their childhood. Perhaps they were rejected by family and society; maybe they were abandoned and neglected by those whom they should have been able to count on. For this reason, they now seek constant validation and reassurance from others. Some may exude the characteristics of a narcissist and may never feel satisfied no matter how much you give to them. They can be selfish, controlling, and very manipulative, injurious to others. As their hearts have grown to be bitter, Satan forms walls of fortification around the bitter roots. Naturally, bitterness attracts and even couples with spirits of witchcraft and manipulation. The people under the influence of these vampire-like spirits often seek comfort, love, and the desire to be nurtured when they are having a weak moment.

At some point, we have all probably carried some of these traits and should seek healing that can only come from a healing Savior, Jesus Christ, who came to heal the brokenhearted.

If you have been guilty of having a sapping taproot yourself, it is time to make an investment into the kingdom of God instead of crying out, "Give to me!" Don't be one of the five foolish virgins who asked to *borrow* the oil of their neighbor.

The time has come and is even now when God is not allowing for a spiritual gray area. A person will conclusively choose life or death, blessing or cursing. There is no longer a place for fence riders or for those who waver back and forth. From God's perspective, every man will either choose to serve Him fully or not at all. For that reason, those who are left outside the walls of the metaphorical city of God should not be pitied because they *refused* to buy the oil to enter the inner court (the bridal chamber). The horseleech will wither in the fire of God's furnace. Its root will be destroyed because of famine. Forevermore, the wicked will be disconnected from the life of God.

The Staggering Effects
of Strong Delusion

Almost everyone would agree that we are living in the days of strong delusion. Jesus prophesied that these days would exist and grow darker in time, especially in the end.

As we have gathered from Jesus's parable of the ten virgins, five were wise, having oil for their lamps in order to see clearly in the end-time. The other five were foolish, in that they had no oil for their lamps wherewith to guide their path. This is tragic because it means they are not going to be able to see during the great deception. In the end, the strong delusion will overtake the people of the night (1 Thess. 5:5), especially as they are separated from the kingdom of light. The wicked will only grow to become darker when the chasm begins to divide the two kingdoms apart from each other (Matt. 13:49). The castaways will be "cast out" to a dimension that scriptures refer to as *outer darkness*. In this detention, darkness exists that is so gross it can be felt! The strong delusion that controls the minds of those walking in darkness is a result of the intoxicating effects of the cup of Babylon.

> Babylon was a gold cup in the LORD's hand; she
> made the whole earth drunk. The nations drank
> her wine; therefore, they have now gone mad.
> (Jer. 51:7)

Scriptures indicate that those who drink from Babylon's cup of harlotries and abominations will partake in her plagues (Rev. 18:4–

5). As a result, they will come under her strong delusion, causing them to sink into a stupor. In other words, her followers will become intoxicated and enter into a deep sleep (trance). Proverbs 4:19 says, "But the way of the wicked is like deep darkness; they do not know what makes them stumble."

Even now, the people of the night are not able to distinguish their right hand from their left (Jon. 4:11). Paul's words to the Romans are still a warning for us today:

> And do this, understanding the present time: The
> hour has already come for you to wake up from
> your slumber, because our salvation is nearer now
> than when we first believed. (Rom. 13:11)

As the two kingdoms are separated into two distinct categories, the followers of Babylon will no longer be allowed to steal the water from the cup of the righteous. Instead, they will be limited to drinking the toxic potion from the cup of Babylon, wherewith comes a staggering delusion that impels men into a deep sleep.

It is evident from the parable that the five foolish virgins are not allowed to steal the oil from the five wise virgins. As a result, they won't be able to see the bridegroom when he arrives. In other words, they will be locked outside the doors of the wedding hall (bridal chamber) (Matt. 25:10).

Isaiah 59:10 says, "We grope like the blind along a wall, feeling our way like people without eyes. Even at brightest noontime, we stumble as though it were dark. Among the living, we are like the dead."

These subjects who are confined to outer darkness will have lacked the oil they needed to keep their lamps burning in the end. Therefore, they're going to be in a state of destitution, groping for the wall like blind men. Destitution is an unfortunate state in which a person lacks something important, like money, food, love, companionship, or even hope.

Destitution is not merely losing a job, going through a divorce, or getting sick. Everyone encounters these negative things in life.

However, not everyone will become destitute, which is being in a state of true hopelessness and despair. Destitution refers to such extreme want that threatens life unless relieved.

There are scriptures in the Bible that speak of men and women in the end who will be turned over to a *strong delusion*. As a result, they will become destitute (lacking some great need[s] in their life that are of great importance). Paul refers to these men as "those who are perishing" and adds to it that they are ensnared in all the ways that wickedness can possibly deceive a man.

These are blind men who "fall for the world," who become ensnared in all of Satan's traps, "for the lust of the eyes; the lust of the flesh; and the pride of life."

> For this reason God sends them a strong delusion
> so that they will believe the lie. (2 Thess. 2:11)

Verse 11 says that God will send them a *strong delusion* so that they will believe all of Satan's lies. They will be in a state of spiritual incoherence where their discernment is nonexistent. However, there must have been a reason for God sending them into strong delusion because Paul writes in the same verse: "For this reason God allowed strong delusion to overtake them."

For what reason does God allow this to happen? If you back up to the last part of the preceding verse (10), Paul writes, "They perish because they refused to love the truth and so be saved."

It was for this reason, "because they refused to love the truth," that God gave them over to deception. They had already made the choice to refuse the truth that would have saved them prior to God releasing them over to their fleshly desires.

What is happening here? Is God, who claims to be long-suffering and rich in mercy, giving up on His created man? Of course not.

It can be related to a parent who has tried everything he knows to help his wayward son. At some point, after all his attempts have failed as a parent, it is time to cut the cord and remove himself *as an enabler* (deterrent, hindrance) in his child's life. Obviously, this doesn't mean removing himself *as a parent*, but at some point, the only thing that can save some people is *rock bottom*. Rock bottom is a place where resources become depleted; a person loses all self-sufficiency and exhausts all efforts of becoming successful in his or her own way.

In a parable, there were repercussions for the prodigal son who turned his back on God to go his own way. Luke 15:13 and 14 say that this young man ran away from his father's house to a distant land. Soon after, a famine hit the particular country where he had settled.

What is the moral lesson hidden for us in this story? When we run from our father's (God's) house to head for a distant country (a place of rebellion, sin, and outer darkness), rest assured that God will send famine (causing destitution) to us in that country. Verse 14 says "he had nothing left" and "he had nothing to live on." He had reached a place of destitution. Verse 14 also says that a severe famine spread throughout that country. Why did a famine strike that particular country? Because that's where his son was located, and he wanted him back home. In order to get us back to a safe place with Him, God will see to it that all our resources are dried up in the areas surrounding us.

Verse 16 says that "no man would give him anything." In this distant place far away from God and in the midst of a dry, hot famine, God will cause our enablers to walk away from us so that we will reach a place where the only place we can look is up. He will remove all self-sufficiency and codependency. No man or woman will give unto us even as we seek them! What a merciful judgment.

Verse 17 says, "He finally came to his senses." Another translation says, "He came to himself." Sometimes the light bulb doesn't come on until we've reached a place called destitution.

This man's *wild living* became more like *low living*. At this point, he would have even been sufficient with eating hog slop in the pigpen. However, he couldn't even get as much as that, so his better judgment finally kicked in.

God will ultimately release us to venture out into a distant country on our own—that is, in order for us to come to the end of ourselves. It is then, only by God's great mercy, that we "come to our senses" and turn our face back to the Father's house. Although it might have been our choice to deviate from the truth, this is the Father's way of having us return to Him after being given over to a strong delusion.

> For this reason God sends them a strong delusion
> so that they will believe the lie. (2 Thess. 2:11)

Let's break down the words *strong delusion* separately so we can better understand the delusion that will be so prevalent in the end.

The word *strong* in Greek is *enérgeia* (energy), which is "power in action, operation, strong, [effectual] working, activity." In the New Testament, it is confined to superhuman activity. In this case, this is in reference to Satan's divine energy (the power with which error works) working within the heart of the wayward. The word *delusion* in Greek is *plánē*, which means "a wandering, error, deviant behavior, a departure from what God says is true, an error [deception] which results in wandering [roaming into sin]." This entails a wandering, a straying about, whereby one, led astray from the right way, roams hither and thither. In the New Testament, it refers to mental straying (i.e., error, wrong opinion relative to morals or religion) *Strong's Concordance*. Therefore, strong delusion refers to the satanic power flowing through an individual that causes him to be led away from what God says is truth into a place of wandering and an error into sin. This is a great deception.

Jesus spoke about those who go astray and lead others astray. He calls them "blind guides" and "bad plants" that will be plucked up.

> Every plant that my heavenly Father has not planted will be pulled up by the roots. They are blind guides leading the blind, and if one blind person guides another, they will both fall into a ditch. (Matt. 15:13–14)

Jude called them "wandering" stars.

> They are wandering stars, for whom blackest
> darkness has been reserved forever. (Jude 1:13)

In this verse, *wandering* in Greek is *planétés*, which, by definition, is "a wanderer, as in a star, or planet [wandering body]." This is figurative for a person who is operating without a spiritual moral compass and exploiting other aimless people, prompting them to also stray from God's circle of truth. This term nearly always conveys the sin of roaming. It is only after people reject God that He allows them to fall under a spell of strong delusion. For this very reason, those who are under strong delusion will be deceived by the working power/activity of the Antichrist spirit when he steps on the global scene.

> The man of sin [The Antichrist] will come with
> the power of Satan. He will use every kind of
> power, including miraculous and wonderful
> signs. But they will be lies. He will use everything
> that God disapproves of to deceive those who are
> dying, those who refused to love the truth that
> would save them. That's why God will send them
> a powerful delusion so that they will believe a lie.
> Then everyone who did not believe the truth, but
> was delighted with what God disapproves of, will
> be condemned. (2 Thess. 2:9–12)

In Paul's letter to the Thessalonian Church, Paul reveals that the deceptive power that will work (operate) so boldly through the Antichrist of the end is already at work, even now, within Satan's human instruments.

Scriptures refer to those who plan and plot how to defile the flesh (and others) as *workers of iniquity*. According to Micah 2:1, iniquity is *planned* and *plotted* or *premeditated* (through the imaginations of wicked men). Hence, they are described as workers of iniquity.

> Woe to those who plan iniquity, to those who plot evil on their beds! At morning's light they carry it out because it is in their power to do it.

These are workmen laboring for an evil kingdom because they habitually practice sin and systematically work to defile themselves and others. David the psalmist prayed,

> Deliver me from those who *work* evil, and save me from bloodthirsty men. (Ps. 59:2)

Here, the psalmist asked God to deliver him from those who practice evil. These are individuals who *work* evil; they have an active (working) flow that carries the power to lure others into sin. This is because demon spirits are involved to entice and seduce the simple (ungrounded). Workers of iniquity are human instruments who make a choice to indulge in immorality, darkness, and injustice. Therefore, the powers (energy) of the evil one actively *work* through them to entice others into darkness. These wicked men are portals of Satan, and the demonic powers working (flowing) through them taint, defile, pollute, corrupt, and stain.

In these last days, individuals who work iniquity and yield themselves to a counterfeit power have been given over to strong delusion. They practice lawlessness (violate God's laws) and are deceived by a mysterious (hidden) allurement to defile the flesh by means of the abominations of the world's temporary pleasures.

The Antichrist has not, as of yet, publicly stepped onto the global scene, yet Paul is saying that *the same spirit* that will operate within the Antichrist is already at work within depraved people (those whom Satan uses as his instruments of defilement). This is Satan's army that defies God in the battle of Armageddon in the end.

In the Bible, Babylon has always represented Satan's kingdom of darkness that lures the world into sin. Notice what the scriptures say about this kingdom: she, Babylon, is drawing darkness to her. She is a home and a hideout for demons.

> He cried out in a loud voice: "She has fallen!
> Great Babylon has fallen! She is now haunted by
> demons and unclean spirits; all kinds of filthy
> and hateful birds live in her." (Rev. 18:2)

Although the supernatural realms are hidden from the natural eye, every kind of demon is welcomed in this spiritual city (kingdom), according to this verse. Take note of the appeal this counterfeit kingdom has. She draws everything abominable, filthy, and hateful. As a matter of fact, demons gravitate to this harlot system because they find it a safe place to make their abode. Although she is the abominable city (and the kingdom of Satan) that is charged with causing people around the globe to sin, individuals who are walking in darkness can also have the same effect on a small-scale personal level. Our bodies are temples that are either a home for demons or a temple of the Holy Spirit. We should not be a dwelling place from which evil entities operate (work) through. Yet the demonic activity that flows through a worker of iniquity creates a seductive appeal that is ready to ensnare its victim into vile sins of the flesh. By nature, their desire is to defile the susceptible in order to bring them into a bond of iniquity with themselves. This is what hell is like, filled with people who are in these bonds.

Just as the wicked allows Satan's power to work within them, God's power can work mightily through the righteous. When writing to the Ephesians, Paul makes known that God is able to do immeasurably more in us than all we could ever ask or imagine, but it is according to His power that is "at work within us."

> God can do great things through us, even beyond
> the imaginable, but it's according to the level of
> power that is *able to work*. (Eph. 3:20)

The questions are these: How much of God's power is a person able to *receive*? How much of God's power are they able to *pour out*? The amount that a man can receive from God will always be a true reflection of the volume he will be able to pour out.

God's power must be *able to work* effectively in us for it to become productive because it's according to the power that *works in us*. If God's power can't move in us, it's not going to be demonstrated. The word *work* in this verse is the Greek word *energeó*, "to be at work, to work, to do." This refers to active, operative energy. When power is working, it is actively operating with the ability to flow, which brings it from one stage (point) to the next, much like an electrical current energizing a wire, bringing it to a shining light bulb (*Strong's Concordance*).

In his second letter to the Thessalonian Church, Paul refers to this currently active (secret) power that lures so many into sin as *the mystery of iniquity*. He writes,

> The mystery of iniquity is already at work. But
> it cannot work effectively until the person now
> holding it back gets out of the way. (2 Thess. 2:7)

Although it is already active, the mysterious spirit of the age cannot work entirely as it would like because the Church is present on the earth to restrain Babylon's powers to some extent. In the verse aforementioned, the word *mystery*, "mystery of iniquity," in Greek is *mustérion*, which means "anything hidden, a secret doctrine, a mystery, secret, of which initiation is necessary" (*Strong's Concordance*).

This is the same hidden power of the occult, defined as "impossible or nearly impossible to see, difficult to see, imperceptible by the eye." Therefore, the mystery of iniquity (of the end) is an occultic power that's currently operating through human instruments who have been given over to strong delusion (to completely indulge in their sins as they so desire). The hidden appeal of darkness leaves an undiscerning heart with an inquiring mind, wondering about its secret mystery. However, it's a dangerous game, and the Church body should be advised to walk away from Lady Folly before their feet get caught in her net.

> Her feet go down to death; her steps head straight
> for Sheol. (Prov. 5:5)

Pay special attention to something mentioned earlier: according to the *Strong's Concordance*, to understand the mystery of iniquity, "initiation is necessary." If you have made vows to an organization or to any other god, law, or doctrine, renounce them now and repent. It's a trap, and to be linked with others who have sworn similar oaths puts you in a bond of iniquity with them. In this case, you have become a victim of Satan's Babylonian slave trade mentioned in the scriptures. The book of Revelation lists "human bodies" and "human souls" as part of Mystery Babylon's slave trade:

> And merchants of the earth will weep and grieve over her [kingdom Babylon], because no one buys their cargo [goods, merchandise] anymore, cinnamon and incense, fragrant oil and frankincense, wine and oil, fine flour and wheat, cattle and sheep, horses and chariots, and the bodies and souls of men. (Rev. 18:11–13)

The mystery of the deceptive alluring power (iniquity) that is currently working can only be revealed by divine revelation, as God unveils it to the Church. It is such a secretive power that it's not made obvious to human understanding. For those walking in darkness (in bonds of iniquity), these are religious (esoteric) secrets that are only revealed to the initiated and not to be communicated by mortals outside the program. The mystery of iniquity is the compelling force that is responsible for many being drawn into the occult (magic)—satanism, the drug culture, the underworld, pornography, human sex trafficking, sexual perversion, adultery, and homosexuality.

The word *iniquity* in *the mystery of iniquity* is the Greek word *anomía* (lawlessness), which means "without law, disobedience, sin." This entails living for self, having no spiritual discipline or parameters, and a condition without any safety walls and boundaries. The word *mystery* refers to a secretively hidden power that is alluring to others.

Iniquity means "complete lawlessness." The *mystery of iniquity*, then, is the hidden spiritual allure that draws the simple into a lifestyle of willful sinning, lawlessness, and depravity. This spirit who poses as some great mystery (to be desired) is already *at work* through those who work iniquity, as they seek to draw others into a common bond of depravity with them. We must be watchful of those who have the power within themselves to corrupt, taint, and defile the human mind and soul, even through vexing conversation. They are vomiters, spewing the world's toxicities. They are like garbage trucks filled with all kinds of smelly garbage. As their garbage piles up, they look for a place to dump it. And if we let them, they'll dump it on us. The world will vomit on us. Just as God has human vessels He pours from, Satan has human portals that his power *works through* to draw others (through the mystery) into aligning with other members of the Babylonian lodge.

God gave me a revelation once of the *vomiting pelican* in Isaiah 34:11. This pelican is symbolic of anyone who overindulges themselves with the world's pleasures as an outlet for the dryness they are encountering in their life. As a result of overindulgence, they become intoxicated and resort to expelling (vomiting) their shame onto others in order to find relief, only to gorge themselves and do it all over again.

Scriptures refer to this intoxicating drink as the Babylonian cup (Rev. 14:8), which is the world's bitter offering to those who are dry and broken in their souls. However, the world has nothing to offer the broken except a bitter cup that defiles and brings great sorrow. All who resort to partaking of her drink will gain great sorrow of regret. We must be on guard: "Bad communication corrupts good morals." As these lawless ones vomit up their evils, even through perverse speech, it can create a breach in our own spirits. The bitter vomitus that they release will leave the smell and residue on those around for them to wrestle with.

The surest way to self-destruct is to accompany bitter people who are in bonds with other like-minded workers of iniquity. These are people in your workplace, church, family, or circle of friends who have intoxicated themselves with the wine of Babylon's fornications and abominations, and now satanic powers actively work through these portals to draw others into the same bond of iniquity as them.

Their own garments are stained with the sins of the flesh, and if God's righteous are left unguarded, they'll be drinking from the same cup of sorrowful regret.

Scripture refers to Satan's kingdom as Mystery Babylon, since Satan uses seductive appeal (mystery) to imprison human souls.

There are two entire chapters in the book of Revelation (chapters 17–18) devoted to the destruction of Babylon. The destruction of this *Mystery* Babylon is clearly described as occurring at the time of the battle of Armageddon, which is the last war of this world between God's kingdom and all those who defy Him. Why is this satanic kingdom in Revelation referred to as Mystery Babylon? There's that word again—*mystery*. What is Mystery Babylon? A mystery is something secret or hidden, a thing that some understand while others do not. Therefore, this spiritual Babylonian kingdom of the end is occult.

> And upon her forehead was a name written, MYSTERY, BABYLON THE GREAT, THE MOTHER OF HARLOTS AND ABOMINATIONS OF THE EARTH. (Rev. 17:5)

In this verse, the word *mystery* is the Greek word *mustérion*, again meaning "anything hidden, a mystery, or secret doctrine of which initiation is necessary." This word comes from a derivative of *muo*, which means "to shut the mouth, a secret or mystery [through the idea of silence imposed by initiation into religious rites]" (*Strong's Concordance*).

The kingdom of darkness always pressures those it enslaves to not share its mystery or secrets as they claim to have such great esoteric knowledge. The initiates of ungodly organizations are no different. They are threatened to keep their mouths shut based on the impositions of the organization's rites they adhere to. It sounds occultic to me! This means that Satan's kingdom here in the last days is going to be a secret society, an occult. The enemy is going to make great attempts to cover up his works of darkness as he imposes his secret agenda to manipulate, intimidate, and dominate. Mystery

Babylon will be subtle and indistinct. She will not reveal her path of death until she has entrapped the souls of her victims.

Babylon in Greek is *Babulón*, which means "gate of god[s]." Babylon, therefore, is a large portal (gate) for demonic entry, involvement, and practice. She is the wide gate that Jesus talked about that leads to destruction.

> Wide is the gate and broad is the way that leads
> to destruction, and many enter through it. (Matt.
> 7:13)

Babylon is the spiritual gate of entry for evil gods or demons. In Revelation 17:5, Babylon the Great is referred to as the "mother of prostitutes and the vile things of the earth." This mysterious kingdom has given birth to moral decay and the abominations that have filled the earth. She has mothered and parented these abominable things that have intoxicated the earth and its inhabitants, the idolatries and moral stench that have reached the nostrils of God. That's why she is called a portal because she is a gateway for this infiltration of iniquity. She is a *habitation* for demons (Rev. 18:2), which means that anyone who is under the influence of her delusion or is used as an individual instrument of her power *serves as a home* for demons and a hideout for every foul vulture and dreadful animal. Those who partake of her cup embody the characteristics of the mother of harlots and abominations (Rev. 17:5).

Let us not be deceived by a compelling desire to know her immoralities. Her fruits are brokenness, emptiness, aimlessness, and wastefulness. Those who drink from her cup will be frozen in time, leading them to great sorrow and regret (weeping and gnashing of teeth) for the things they didn't have the time to do.

The mystery of iniquity is synonymous with the deadly allure of the evil tree in the Garden of Eden. However, we mustn't be enticed by its hidden and enticing allure. Her fruits are death!

Even now, the strong delusion that comes from this present age is currently at work in the world we now live in. Because those who *wandered away* rejected the truth in former times, they will be deceived and believe what is counterfeit in the latter days, especially in the end when deception is at its highest point. However, it wasn't too late for the prodigal son in Jesus's story, and it's not too late to turn back now. Upon seeing his son return, the father's own words were, "My son was dead and has come back to life. He was lost but has been found" (Luke 15:24).

The demonic powers of delusion had been broken off his son's life as he turned his face back toward his father's house. He left the path of brokenness, wandering, and destitution for a crown in his own home with his true family, his family in Christ.

For us who are alive today, we mustn't wait till it's too late to cut ties with members of darkness. We will be likened to the foolish virgins who tried to borrow the oil because they didn't want to break away from the other fools around them. The mysterious pull toward darkness is not being truthful. Its end is death and destruction.

The Elijah Mantle on the
Two Witnesses

Throughout the course of Bible history, particularly since John's revelations on the isle of Patmos, there has been much debate about who the two witnesses of Revelation 11 will be. Many Bible scholars predict that Moses and Elijah satisfy the conditions required for these end-time ministries because they will use the elements of nature to consume their foes (Rev. 11:5). This includes, but is not limited to, the use of fire that corresponds with Elijah's ministry:

> But Elijah replied to the captain, "If I am a man of God, let fire come down from heaven and destroy you and your fifty men!" Then fire fell from heaven and killed them all. (2 Kings 1:10)

Revelation 11:6 says that the two end-time prophets will also have the power to shut up the heavens so that it will not rain during the time they are prophesying, to turn the waters into blood, and to strike the earth with every kind of plague as often as they want.

Again, this agrees with the ministries of the Old Testament prophets Moses and Elijah.

Even the New Testament writer James wrote about Elijah having the same power over the elements of the weather as the two witnesses will have. James 5:17 says, "Elijah was a man just like us. He prayed earnestly that it would not rain, and it did not rain on the land for three and a half years."

When Moses was battling the oppressive system of the Egyptian kingdom, he actually turned the Nile waters into blood (Exod. 7:20). In addition, God used him to administer judgment through the ten plagues that devastated the entire land of Egypt (Exod. 1–12).

Is it any wonder, then, why Bible scholars and believers alike would surmise that the two most noteworthy Old Testament prophets would "fit the bill" for the Revelation 11 end-time witnesses? The similitude of their ministries seems irrefutable.

Elijah was a prophet who appeared out of nowhere. His appearance in 1 Kings 17 signaled a new era in the history of Israel. He was one of the forerunners of prophetic judgment, and as Moses did with the Egyptian pharaoh, Elijah dealt somewhat harshly with those in administrative headquarters (Ahab and Jezebel).

Elijah lived in a "God's prophets versus the pagan prophets" dispensation of time. He was a crisis profit, also known as the troubler of Israel, first appearing in Ahab's palace prophesying drought and famine. It wouldn't be long until he was on top of Mount Carmel calling fire down from heaven, which destroyed the false prophets of Baal. As he stood in the office of a prophet, God used him to administer justice and declare judgment against the idolatry in the land.

Why did Elijah pray earnestly for a famine to strike the land? Where's the fun, make-me-feel-good stuff? Why didn't the man of God pray for things like love, prosperity, favor, and promotion? On God's time clock, there are specific dispensations of time that God appoints, even for judgment. Judgment is an act of God's love, preserving some from the fires of the blazing furnace that is to come.

God is preparing His bride for His Son's return. As the God of the harvest begins to separate the wheat from the tares in these last days, more of God's end-time *"Elijahs"* (prophets) will arise to make similar declarations. As a matter of fact, the Elijah mantle is a spiritual concept that, if understood, will help decipher the Revelation 11 mystery of the two witnesses. So then what is the Elijah mantle?

Elijah's personal journey with God was an ascension. It had drawn him upward to a very high spiritual dimension. Scriptures indicate that Elijah was translated to heaven by the chariots of God.

His story is unique as he was caught up by a whirlwind and taken to heaven without experiencing death.

Prior to his translation, Elijah had faithfully groomed Elisha, the prophet who would succeed him, for ministry. As a matter of fact, the anointing of Elijah's life was so powerful and unique that God asked him to "pass the torch," so to speak, to the next generation of prophets. God specifically assigned Elijah to anoint or "impart" his prophetic anointing to other prophets along his spiritual journey.

> Then the LORD told him [Elijah], "Go back the same way you came, and travel to the wilderness of Damascus. When you arrive there, anoint Hazael to be king of Aram. Then anoint Jehu, grandson of Nimshi to be king of Israel, and anoint Elisha son of Shaphat from the town of Abel-meholah to replace you as my prophet." (1 Kings 19:15–16)

Hence, the passing down of Elijah's mantle is a spiritual concept used to describe the transference of the anointing that was on Elijah to the succeeding generations of prophets. Elisha the pupil accompanied his lord Elijah on his spiritual journey from Gilgal to Bethel, Bethel to Jericho, and Jericho to the Jordan River before the mantle was dropped (and the anointing was transferred).

Just prior to his translation, Elijah said to Elisha,

> "Tell me what I can do for you before I am taken away." Elisha replied, "Please let me inherit a double portion of your spirit [anointing] and become your successor." (2 Kings 2:9)

And as they continued along and talked, a chariot of fire with horses of fire appeared suddenly and separated the two of them, and Elijah went up to heaven in a whirlwind. Scriptures indicate that Elisha then *picked up the mantle that had fallen down from Elijah* and went back and stood on the bank of the Jordan. He took the mantle of Elijah and struck the waters and said, "Where is the LORD, the God of Elijah?" And when he, too, had struck the waters, they divided this way and that, and Elisha crossed over. Notice that Elisha had not performed a miracle until after the mantle of Elijah had fallen on him.

Second Kings 2:15 says that when the group of prophets from Jericho saw from a distance what had happened, they exclaimed, "Elijah's spirit rests upon Elisha!" Herein lies the meaning behind the Elijah mantle falling on God's prophets who seek His anointing. Perhaps it is metaphorical that Elijah never experienced death. His spirit could live on through the prophets who succeeded him thereafter. His mantle could be transferred from one prophet to the next as the Spirit of God that was on Elijah (to do great miracles) would never die; it would continue to be alive forevermore. "Elijah's spirit rested upon Elisha," scriptures say. In other words, the same anointing that was on Elijah came upon Elisha. There would be many Elijahs thereafter because the anointing on him for the prophetic office would always transfer to those who were willing to make the journey for the golden oil (from Gilgal to Jordan), the same journey that Elisha took to lay hold of it.

In his journey from Gilgal to Jordan, the ministry of Elijah involved the "shedding of light." In pouring out the golden oil from within himself, he was allowing his light to shine among men, one in particular, Elisha. In essence, Elisha was saying, "Elijah, show me the way to the golden oil. Lead me to the hundredfold path." In the character of a true shepherd, Elijah brought light to the path that Elisha would follow in his quest for the golden oil, the double portion anointing.

Enlightening the path for others to obtain the oil (anointing) is a ministry filled with the greatest of rewards. Will you accept the call to become an Elijah? Will you embrace the journey (of brokenness) so that you might obtain the power of impartation and the ability to quicken the gifts and callings of God within others? The spirit of Elijah will rest on you as it did with Elisha. More importantly, it will light upon the two witnesses for the purpose of ministry involving the powerful elements of nature. Will you glory in tribulation knowing that the mastery of such tests will allow you to drop your mantle to the next Elisha? Will you partake in the sufferings of Christ so that you may also rejoice when His glory is revealed (1 Pet. 4:13)?

Elijah was one of the two prototypes (the other being Moses) that God used to describe the two witnesses, whose ministries will bring oil during the tribulation. The ministry of Elijah in the Old Testament was (and is) a foreshadow of the two witnesses of Revelation 11 who will be appointed to minister to the world before Christ's return. As Elijah led Elisha on his quest for the anointing, the two witnesses will lead the Church to the golden oil in the last days before the return of Christ. They will serve as Elijahs who lead the journey (metaphorically from Gilgal to Jordan) and will drop down their mantles to the world as they depart to heaven in a cloud.

> Then a loud voice from heaven called to the
> two prophets, "Come up here!" And they rose
> to heaven in a cloud as their enemies watched.
> (Rev. 11:12)

They will depart from this earth in the same fashion as Elijah, who was caught up to heaven in a whirlwind! Some of those who are left behind will, like Elisha, pick up their mantles and begin doing miracles themselves in Jesus's name. The signs and wonders that will be demonstrated through the testimony of the two witnesses in the end-time are comparable to those that followed Elijah (i.e., ministering with fire, shutting up the heavens so it doesn't rain).

When Christ returns, there will be two types of people who are caught up in glory to be joined with him: those who are "alive and remain" and those who are "dead in Christ." Elijah is representative of the first group of people who are alive on the earth when Christ returns. They will rise (often referred to as the rapture) to be with the Lord, as Elijah was, without experiencing death.

> After that, we who are alive and remain will be
> caught up together with them in the clouds to
> meet the Lord in the air. (1 Thess. 4:17)

Moses is the other prototype whose ministry serves as an example of the two witnesses that will bring oil during the tribulation (turning water into blood and striking the earth will all types of plagues as often as they wish) (Rev. 11:6). While Elijah represents those who are alive and taken to heaven, Moses represents those who have experienced death yet rise to meet their maker.

> For the Lord himself will come down from heaven, with a loud command, with the voice of the archangel and with the trumpet call of God, and the dead in Christ will rise first. (1 Thess. 4:16)

Both Moses and Elijah were present with Jesus on the Mount of Transfiguration. The appearance of these two Old Testament figures was significant. Moses was symbolic of the Old Testament law since God revealed the Ten Commandments to His people through him. Elijah represented the Old Testament prophets since he was the mentor for a school of prophets. On the mountain that day, God's voice from heaven rang out, "This is My Son. Listen to Him!" This was God clearly confirming to the three eyewitnesses (Peter, James, and John) that the law and the prophets must give way to Jesus for a new and better covenant in His Son's blood. In 2 Corinthians 13:1, Paul said that nothing will stand firm in court without the testimony of two or three people (witnesses).

Every matter must be established by the testimony of two or three witnesses.

Here, in the presence of three witnesses (Peter, James, and John), the mediator of the new and living covenant, Jesus, was replacing the old. God was putting His stamp of approval upon His Son, forever sealing this truth, as the story would be told and retold to all until His return. He was the fulfillment of both the law and the innumerable prophecies in the Old Testament.

In the same fashion that Elijah led Elisha toward the (double portion) anointing—from Gilgal, Bethel, Jericho, and Jordan—so the ministry will be of the two witnesses who are mentioned in the book of Revelation. They will bring oil to God's people (the true virgin bride) who remain on the earth.

In the former days, oil was needed to keep lamps burning. Without oil, there would be no light to see by. God had spoken of the gross darkness at the end of times.

> See, darkness covers the earth and thick darkness
> is over the peoples. (Isa. 60:2)

After Elijah was taken up, his spirit remained transferrable. Elijah's mantle has since fallen on other men, for one, John the Baptist. Through the Old Testament prophet Malachi, God prophesied that "Elijah" would return someday (Mal. 4:5–6). However, this reference to Elijah in the book of Malachi was actually fulfilled through the personage of John the Baptist, who would minister with the same anointing (spirit) that rested on Elijah (and then Elisha). Through the prophet Malachi, God spoke, saying,

> Behold, I will send you Elijah the prophet before
> the great and awesome day of the Lord comes.
> And he will turn the hearts of fathers to their chil-
> dren and the hearts of children to their fathers,
> lest I come and strike the land with a decree of
> utter destruction. (Mal. 4:5–6)

Even today, many people (according to custom) take this scripture literally and are still expecting the arrival of the Old Testament Elijah because of God's promise in this verse: "I will send you Elijah." They even include an empty chair at the table in anticipation that Elijah will return to herald the Messiah in fulfillment of Malachi's word.

The disciples of Jesus were confused about the prophecy in Malachi—the return of Elijah—so they asked Him, "Why do the scribes say that Elijah must return before the Messiah comes?" (Matt. 7:10). Jesus revealed that John the Baptist *was* the "Elijah" mentioned in Malachi 4, thus fulfilling Malachi's prophecy already. Jesus answered and said to his disciples,

> Indeed, Elijah is coming first and will restore all things. But I tell you, Elijah has already come, but he wasn't recognized, and they chose to abuse him. And in the same way they will also make the Son of Man suffer. (Matt. 17:11–12)

Notice what Jesus said here: "Elijah has already come, but he wasn't recognized." Additionally, Matthew 17:13 says,

> Then the disciples realized he [Jesus] was talking about John the Baptist.

Jesus spoke even more plainly concerning John, saying,

> And if you are willing to accept it, he [John the Baptist] is the Elijah who was to come. (Matt. 11:14)

Although the Elijah spirit rested on John the Baptist, who was a forerunner to Christ's "first" appearance, the Elijah mantle will also be on the two witnesses who will be the forerunners for Christ's "reappearance" (Second Coming). God sent messengers that preceded Him the first time, and the two witnesses are the messengers that will precede His return.

Like John, the two witnesses will have the Elijah mantle upon them when they start their testimonies.

> And I will give unto my two witnesses, and they shall prophesy a thousand two hundred and threescore days [three and a half years], clothed in sackcloth. (Rev. 11:3)

God is going to empower them for a ministry that in many ways resembles the ministries of Moses and Elijah. Many people are literal in their beliefs about the two witnesses. They are convinced that the two Old Testament prophets are going to return from heaven in person. However, the two witnesses are going to be two people who are already alive on the earth at the end of days when these things appear. They will be walking in the office of a prophet and in the power of Elijah to "restore all things" (Matt. 17:11), because the Elijah mantle comes with an anointing that "restores."

> Then the disciples asked Him, saying, "Why then do the scribes say that Elijah must come first?" Jesus answered and said to them, "Indeed, Elijah is coming first and will restore all things."
> (Matt. 17:10–11)

Will the actual Old Testament Elijah (and Moses) come again to restore all things? Certainly not. The end-time "Elijah anointing" is reserved for God's two prophets of Revelation 11 who are being prepared for the miraculous, even now.

The two witnesses will assist in bringing about the "final restoration" of kingdom things. What is the final restoration of all things? In Acts, when Peter stood up in the temple, he spoke to the people about the "final restoration" of things, which will be in the end:

> Then times of refreshment will come from the presence of the Lord, and he will again send you Jesus, your appointed Messiah. For he [Jesus] must remain in heaven until the time for the final restoration of all things, as God promised long ago through his holy prophets. (Acts 3:20–21)

The Old Testament describes this restoration in several places, including the relationships between fathers and children.

> His [Elijah's] preaching will turn the hearts of
> fathers to their children, and the hearts of chil-
> dren to their fathers. Otherwise I will come and
> strike the land with a curse. (Mal. 4:6)

According to this verse, the reason for Elijah's return was (and will be again) to "turn the hearts" of fathers and their children back toward one another. In other words, the role of the two witnesses will be "peacemakers," their goal reconciliation. They will not only turn the hearts of men toward God but the hearts of families back to one another.

Although John the Baptist was the "metaphorical" Elijah who called people to repentance, prepared them for the coming of Jesus Christ, and established the ministry of reconciliation (2 Cor. 5:18), anyone on whom the Elijah mantle rests upon will have the anointing (and the authority) to do the same for their generations.

> Everything is from God, who has reconciled us
> to himself through Christ and has given us the
> ministry of reconciliation. (2 Cor. 5:18)

Relationships will be restored, and the hearts of the offended will be healed. The day that is coming will burn like a furnace (Mal. 4:1), and everything that offends will be taken out of the way (cast out) (Matt. 13:41). Why? Because God is sending Elijah once again to restore all things:

> Look, I will send you Elijah the prophet before
> the great and awesome day of the LORD comes.
> He will lead children and parents to love each
> other more, so that when I come, I won't bring
> destruction to the land. (Mal. 4:5–6)

The two witnesses will restore the temple of God so that He can dwell with His people forever. John the Revelator saw the holy city, the New Jerusalem, coming down out of heaven from God, made ready as a bride adorned for her husband:

> And I heard a great voice out of the throne saying, Behold, the tabernacle of God is with men, and he shall dwell with them, and they shall be his peoples, and God himself shall be with them, and be their God. (Rev. 21:2)

The temple that Jesus came to build was different in that it was invisible, not made with men's hands.

Some Pharisees asked Jesus when God's kingdom would come. He answered,

> God's kingdom isn't something you can see. There is no use saying, "Look! Here it is" or "Look! There it is." God's kingdom is within you. (Luke 17:21)

Zerubbabel and Joshua, who were given the assignment to build the second temple, were Old Testament "types" and "shadows" of the two witnesses of Revelation. God revealed these things to the Old Testament prophet Zechariah. Zechariah had a vision of these things as far back as the sixth century BC. The two witnesses (in the form of Zerubbabel and Joshua) were prophetically spoken about even before Jesus made His appearance on earth!

> Then I [Zechariah] asked the angel, "What are these two olive trees on the right and the left of the lampstand?" Again I asked him, "What are these two olive branches beside the two gold pipes that pour out golden oil?" He replied, "Do you not know what these are?" "No, my lord," I said. So he said, "These are the two who are anointed to serve the Lord of all the earth." (Zech. 4:11–14)

Although Zerubbabel and Joshua would build the Old Testament temple made with man's hands (in Zechariah's time), they were foreshadowings whose ministries parallel God's two end-time prophets. The two witnesses in the end will put the final capstone on the unseen temple (Church), which is Christ's body. Jesus came to the earth to build a spiritual temple, which He spoke of when Peter received the revelation of Christ as Messiah. Jesus spoke, saying,

> Now I say to you that you are Peter [which means "rock"], and upon this rock I will build my church, and the gates of hell will not conquer it. (Matt. 16:18)

Peter was one of the many rocks that Christ would use as material to build His spiritual temple here on earth. The Messiah's words were, "I will build My Church." And just as Zerubbabel put the final capstone on the temple that was constructed with man's hands, the two witnesses will put the final piece on the spiritual temple of Christ.

> What are you, O great mountain [of obstacles]? Before Zerubbabel [who will rebuild the temple] you will become a plain [insignificant]! And he will bring out the capstone [of the new temple] with loud shouts of "Grace, grace to it!" (Zech. 4:7)

The two witnesses will bring the same building plan to finish the New Testament Church. In the same way that John the Revelator was instructed to measure the temple—because he brought the final book (Revelation) to the Church—the two witnesses will (similarly) be given a measuring instrument with instructions on "how to" finish its construction:

> And a measuring rod like a staff was given to me, saying, "Rise and measure the temple of God,

and the altar, and those worshipping in it." (Rev. 11:1)

These two prophets will be two people who are alive on the earth in conjunction with when the Antichrist makes his appearance. They will come in the same anointing as Moses and Elijah, and like Elijah, they will have the authority to impart revelation, transfer the anointing, and drop their mantles to others when they depart. They will pour out of themselves the golden oil, which will give the light necessary to bring about the "final restoration" of kingdom things.

The Gnashing of Teeth

In Christianity, the exterior darkness or "outer darkness" is a place into which a person may be "cast out" and where there is "weeping and gnashing of teeth." Although the outer darkness mentioned in the New Testament has generally been thought of as eternal hell, it refers more to a place of separation from God and from the metaphorical "wedding banquet" that Jesus is expected to have upon His Second Coming.

After studying the three parables in the gospel of Matthew, outer darkness is obviously a place of judgment reserved for godless men. The phrase "gnashing of teeth" is linked to the outer darkness in all three of these accounts. However, there are many other places in the scripture where "gnashing of teeth" is used. Let's first find out more about what might cause a person (that has been excluded) to gnash their teeth.

Jesus used a parable to illustrate the nature of the end-time and the separation that will occur between good and evil. He taught, saying,

> As therefore the tares are gathered and burned
> in the fire; so shall it be in the end of this world.
> The Son of man shall send forth his angels, and
> they shall gather out of his kingdom all things
> that offend, and them which do iniquity; And
> shall cast them into a furnace of fire: there shall
> be wailing and gnashing of teeth. Then shall the
> righteous shine forth as the sun in the kingdom
> of their Father. (Matt. 13:40–43)

This parable is teeming with end-time symbolism! In the Bible, the tares represent wicked men (those who work iniquity). Jesus explained this in the preceding verses, saying,

> The field is the world, the good seeds are the sons of the kingdom, but the tares are the sons of the wicked one. (Matt. 13:38)

Jesus explained that the tares would be gathered together, even tied in a bundle, to be burned in a furnace of fire, unable to infiltrate (hinder) the righteous assembly any longer!

> Let both [the wheat and the tares] grow together until the harvest, and at the time of harvest I will say to the reapers, "First gather together the tares and bind them in bundles to burn them, but gather the wheat into my barn." (Matt. 13:30)

At this juncture, there will be a *gathering together* of the righteous and a *gathering out* of the stumbling blocks. Verse 41 says that the Son of Man shall send forth His angels, and they shall *gather out* of His kingdom all things that offend and them who do iniquity.

Jesus shared yet another parable to illustrate the process used for gathering up the wicked and casting them out into the furnace of fire (outer darkness). He likened the filtering method to a fisherman who took the fish from a net—he kept the good fish and cast out the bad:

> Again, the kingdom of heaven is like unto a net, that was cast into the sea, and gathered of every kind: Which, when it was full, they drew to shore, and sat down, and gathered the good into vessels, but cast the bad away. So shall it be at the end of the world: the angels shall come forth, and sever the wicked from among the just, And shall cast them into the furnace of fire: there shall be wailing and gnashing of teeth. (Matt. 13:47–50)

"So shall it be at the end of the world," Jesus declared. These are the days that we now live. Verse 49 says the angels will actually "sever" the wicked from among the just.

Fire Causes Men to Gnash Their Teeth

What is it about this separation (filtering process) that causes the excluded members to gnash their teeth? The passage of scripture in Matthew 13 notes that all who oppose the construction of Christ's Church shall be cast into the furnace of fire. The blazing furnace, wherewith the wicked will be thrown, will cause excruciating anguish (soul pain).

Imagine the reaction a person makes when he accidentally burns himself on a hot stove. The immediate reaction is to clench his teeth together because the pain is so bad. This furnace of fire is a refining wilderness heat indeed!

I can draw from a personal dating experience I once had. After a few years of being in a toxic relationship with a particular man, I recall feeling like the torment I encountered was so intense that it was burning me on the inside and out. The best way I can describe it is that it was hell on earth. What a fiery torment it was, indeed, until I cut the cord with this man! I would later discover that he was one of Satan's workers (of iniquity) and involved in occult (underground) activity. As a result of my involvement with him, I have come to know the meaning behind a torment so severe that it can cause a man to gnash his teeth.

Jesus's purpose for appearing on the earth was to bring fire because fire causes separation. Jesus said,

> I came to bring fire on the earth, and how I wish
> it were already set ablaze! Do you think that I
> came here to give peace to the earth? No, I tell
> you, but rather division! (Luke 12:49, 51)

Fire is paramount to the separation of the wheat and the tares in the end. It is also the element necessary to *sever* a man's God-given purpose from the idols in his heart. Before we can be sent out to subdue kingdoms and expand horizontally, our faith must first be tried by fire (1 Pet. 1:7). Therefore, God's fire is a delivering fire that purifies our faith!

> For he will be like a blazing fire that refines metal, or like a strong soap that bleaches clothes. He will sit like a refiner of silver, burning away the dross. (Mal. 3:2–3)

The fire of God also burns away any dead attachments in the form of associations and relationships with toxic people (workers of iniquity). As we learned from the parable of Jesus, the heat from the famine severed the prodigal son from his enablers and drove him back to his father's house.

The Holy Ghost fire upon Jesus's ministry created hostility from an opposing kingdom of darkness that caused men to "gnash their teeth" upon Him. Therefore, knowing that Christ was hated because of the fire, the world will also hate His body the same. Jesus said, "If the world hates you, know that it has hated me before it hated you" (John 15:18). First John 3:13 says to not be surprised that the world hates you. We should rejoice in our persecutions, knowing that we are surrounded by a great cloud of witnesses, for they (evil men) gnashed their teeth on the prophets of old in like manner:

> Blessed are those who are persecuted for righteousness' sake, for theirs is the kingdom of heaven. Blessed are you when others revile you and persecute you and utter all kinds of evil against you falsely on my account. Rejoice and be glad, for your reward is great in heaven, for so they persecuted the prophets who were before you. (Matt. 5:10–12)

Undoubtedly, the fire of God will create a backlash from the wicked. In Paul's day, this fire even drove the animals to react with hostility against him. When Paul stoked the fire on the island of Malta, scriptures indicate that a snake was driven out by the heat.

> As Paul gathered an armful of sticks and was lay-
> ing them on the fire, a poisonous snake, driven
> out by the heat, bit him on the hand. (Acts 28:3)

Likewise, our spiritual life should be so hot as to cause demons to manifest themselves! As the members of the body of Christ begin to walk in this same fire (authority), demons (in the form of men) will gnash their teeth on them in rage.

Unforgiveness Causes Men to Gnash Their Teeth

The spirit of unforgiveness is another reason for a man to gnash his teeth as he is cast out into the torments of outer darkness. Jesus taught a parable about an unforgiving servant who was forgiven of all his debt. Having compassion for him, the king showed mercy and excused him of all he owed. After he went out, this same servant found a fellow servant who owed him money. Instead of having pity on him, he threw him in prison until he repaid the debt. When the king heard of this, he was enraged and called for the unforgiving servant. It is interesting what happened as a result. Verse 34 says the king "handed him over to the tormentors." Jesus finished the story, saying,

> This is how my heavenly Father will treat each of
> you unless you forgive your brother or sister from
> your heart. (Matt. 18:35)

When a person harbors unforgiveness toward his fellow man, God will cast him into outer darkness by handing him over to the *tormentors* (demon spirits), hence another cause for a man to gnash his teeth.

God's furnace is a place of His all-consuming fire. And because the heat will be so intense, the wicked will become stubble, leaving them neither root nor branch! God prophesied these things through His Old Testament prophet Malachi, saying,

> Surely the day is coming; it will burn like a furnace. All the arrogant and every evildoer will be stubble, and the day that is coming will set them on fire, says the Lord Almighty. Not a root or a branch will be left to them. But for you who revere my name, the sun of righteousness will rise with healing in its rays. And you will go out and frolic like well-fed calves. Then you will trample on the wicked; they will be ashes under the soles of your feet on the day when I act, says the Lord Almighty. Remember the law of my servant Moses, the decrees and laws I gave him at Horeb for all Israel. See, I will send the prophet Elijah to you before that great and dreadful day of the Lord comes. He will turn the hearts of the parents to their children, and the hearts of the children to their parents; or else I will come and strike the land with total destruction. (Mal. 4:1–6)

There is coming a day ("surely the day is coming") when the fire of God will be so hot through the medium of the Church that it will be as if men ("all the arrogant and every evildoer") are thrown into a furnace and burned. "It will burn like a furnace!" scriptures say.

Jealousy Causes Men to Gnash Their Teeth

Although the wicked gnash their teeth from the anguishing fires of torment, soul pain, and unforgiveness, boiling jealousy is also responsible for causing the wicked to gnash their teeth on the righteous. Ezekiel 8 describes a specific idol (demon) that was placed in God's temple, which actually "provoked God to jealousy."

> So I [Ezekiel] lifted up my eyes to the north, and
> in the entrance north of the Altar Gate I saw this
> idol of jealousy. (Ezek. 8:5)

The religious elders of Israel were worshipping idols in God's temple, which provoked jealousy within God. If idolatrous people can provoke God to jealousy, then surely they have the ability to do the same to His people. Satan works tirelessly to offend the righteous in order to evoke within them envy and jealousy toward evildoers.

God spoke to the prophet Ezekiel, saying,

> Son of man, He said to me, do you see what the
> elders of the house of Israel are doing in the dark-
> ness, each at the shrine of his own idol? For they
> are saying, "The LORD does not see us; the LORD
> has forsaken the land." (Ezek. 8:12)

The elders were religious men who spent time in God's temple. The abominable acts committed in secret were stirring God to jealous anger.

Satan causes the same emotions to boil within the members of the body of Christ. If we are not careful, workers of iniquity will create pitfalls of offense that cause the righteous to gnash their teeth out of (jealous) emulations. However, the psalmist encouraged us not to be jealous of workers of iniquity when they seem to be winning the wrong way:

> Do not fret when wicked men seem to succeed!
> Do not envy evildoers! For they will quickly dry
> up like grass, and wither away like plants. (Ps.
> 37:1–2)

So then knowing that Satan is working overtime to cause the righteous to gnash their teeth in jealousy toward evildoers, we should be aware of the scheme he uses, which is the bait of offense.

When God's people avoid these pitfalls and remain free from bitter offenses, the wind will shift directions. It will be the wicked who begin gnashing their teeth out of a jealous rage toward those who walk upright before God.

This degree of jealousy was present in Joseph's brothers. They were so jealous of the favor on Joseph's life that they faked his death and sold him for twenty shekels to a caravan of Ishmaelites who took him to Egypt as a slave (Gen. 37).

God gave Joseph many dreams, and as he shared the dreams with his family, Joseph's brothers would gnash their teeth at him. Genesis 37:5 says, "Joseph had a dream, and when he told it to his brothers, they hated him all the more."

Verse 8 continues, "His brothers said to him, Do you intend to reign over us? Will you actually rule us? And they hated him because of his dream and what he had said."

Genesis 37:11 says, "His brothers were jealous of him."

Jealousy is an evil monster and is one of the many reasons why men in outer darkness gnash their teeth upon God's people. In Psalm 112:10, the psalmist writes (with emphasis added), "The wicked man sees it [the good deeds of the righteous] and is angry; he gnashes his teeth and melts away; the desire of the wicked will perish!"

And then in Psalm 37:12–13, "The wicked person schemes against the righteous and gnashes his teeth at him. The Lord laughs at him because he sees that his day is coming."

David encountered this himself, saying, "Like profane mockers at a feast, they gnash at me with their teeth" (Ps. 35:16).

When wicked men refuse to harness their jealousies toward the righteous, they will begin to act out openly. Jealousy can only be suppressed for so long until it has to manifest, revealing itself in its real light. Jealousy will take a person so far as to even drive a man to snuff his enemy's light out.

Lamentations 2:16 says, "All your enemies open their mouths against you. They hiss and gnash their teeth, saying, 'We have swallowed her up. This is the day we have waited for! We have lived to see it.'"

In the Old Testament, a spirit of jealousy caused King Saul to gnash his teeth at David, the shepherd boy. After David slew the giant (Goliath), the Jewish women were dancing in a victory parade, singing:

> Saul has slain his thousands, and David his tens
> of thousands. (1 Sam. 18:7)

Because the people made more of David's one victory than Saul's many, the king went into rage and became jealous of the young leader.

> What's this? Saul said. They credit David with
> ten thousands and me with only thousands. Next
> they'll be making him their king! So from that
> time on Saul kept a jealous eye on David. (1 Sam.
> 18:8–9)

At this juncture and from that moment on, King Saul plotted to kill David. Instead of leading his country, King Saul wasted his time chasing David in an attempt to murder him.

The very next day, scriptures indicate that a *tormenting spirit* from God overwhelmed Saul, and he began to rave in his house like a madman. David was playing the harp, as he did each day, but Saul had a spear in his hand and suddenly hurled it at David, intending to pin him to the wall. But David escaped him twice. Although David stayed faithful to the king, 1 Samuel 18:29 says that Saul remained David's enemy for the rest of his life.

Truth Causes Men to Gnash Their Teeth

According to a written account in Acts, the penetrating power of truth coupled with wisdom caused men who were influenced by religious spirits to gnash their teeth on one of Christ's leading disciples. In Acts 7, the truth of Stephen's speech infuriated the religious men of that day, causing the Sanhedrin to stop up their ears and gnash their teeth at him (Acts 7:54, 57). Their rage was so elevated and uncontrollable that they took extreme measures by stoning him! The word *gnash* in Acts 7:54 is *bruchó*, which means "to grind the teeth for rage or pain."

The religious leaders gnashed their teeth on the anointed man of God because they rejected the truth that would have otherwise saved them. These are wicked, defiled, and profane men, scoffers, mockers, enemies of God's people, and workers of iniquity.

Religious people are often haughty and unteachable. Proud men are in opposition to God, scriptures declare; in turn, God opposes them (James 4:6). Similarly, the spirit of pride caused Lucifer to gnash his teeth on his creator.

> Your heart became proud on account of your beauty, and you corrupted your wisdom because of your splendor. (Ezek. 28:17)

The psalmist declared in Psalm 2:1–5 that the heathen rages or gnashes their teeth against the Lord and His anointed.

> Why do the heathen rage, and the people imagine a vain thing? The kings of the earth set themselves, and the rulers take counsel together, against the Lord, and against his anointed, saying, Let us break their bands asunder, and cast away their cords from us. He that sitteth in the heavens shall laugh: the Lord shall have them in derision. Then shall he speak unto them in his wrath, and vex them in his sore displeasure.

Verse 2 makes mention of how proud men on the earth "set themselves against the Lord" and against His anointed. The words *set themselves* is the Greek word *yatsab*, a verb that means "to set or station oneself, take one's stand." This is an example of the proud and evil heart defying God (and the inward aboding of His Spirit). Why do they take a stance against God and His anointed? The next verse answers that for us. They say, "Let us break their bands asunder and cast away their cords from us."

As God's Spirit begins to move in the heart of the ungodly, they resist the inner promptings and defiantly "set themselves" against Him. They array themselves for battle against God and against His anointed ones. Their mission is to remain in darkness as they stiff-heartedly oppose the internal promptings of God's prophetic word when He speaks in regard to the idols in their lives.

How does God respond to their defiant and rebellious acts? Although Psalm 2 reveals the prideful man who resists God, James 4:6 says it goes both ways: "God resists the proud, but giveth grace unto the humble." There is definitely a battle that rages between God and the proud of heart who stand up to oppose Him. These scriptures are merely proof of this truth.

The word *resist*, "God resists the proud," is a very old military term, which was used for placing a soldier in a specific platoon (with a specific function) (i.e., in a definite order to attack or resist). Accordingly, it is used in antiquity of organized resistance, like an army assuming a specific battle-array position to resist in "full alignment," to disagree (oppose) intensely. This is such an accurate portrayal of God's method for dealing with the proud. He resists the wicked by aligning His intercessors in a specific battle-array position to do target prayers in order to bind and oppose the powers that work through the proud of heart. Praying intercessors are God's instruments for releasing judgment. Jesus said, "Whatever you bind on earth will be bound in heaven" (Matt. 18:18). It is the members of the body of Christ who are to bind the wicked and cast them out into the blazing fires of outer darkness. These are merciful acts of preserving judgment on behalf of the ungodly.

As the body of Christ comes into a revealed knowledge of how to effectively pray, she will begin to bind those who are instruments of arrogance and pride. A person who understands how to pray can cause the sorcerer to close shop. The prayer of binding will paralyze the effectiveness and limit the influence of the heathen. As a result, he will be brought low.

We are called to be restrainers in this life because we are children of the Restrainer. As a matter of fact, Paul reveals that even the Antichrist cannot be revealed until the appointed time because "the restrainer" is holding him back.

> And you know what [the Church] is now restraining him [the Antichrist], so that he will be revealed at the proper time. (2 Thess. 2:6; brackets added for emphasis)

The word *restrains* in this verse is the Greek word *katechó*, which means "to hold fast, hold back, bind, restrain."

Paul continued further into verse 7, saying, "For this lawlessness is already at work secretly, and it will remain secret until the one who is holding it back steps out of the way."

Satan is thrashing about, and his rage will always manifest through his human workers. These instruments of evil who emanate bitterness and rage are small stones (stumbling blocks) who gnash their teeth at the righteous because they are trying to change the set times in the end. However, they will not be able to "break the bands asunder," scriptures declare, or "cast away their cords" (Ps. 2) because they are bound and cast out!

Rock of Offense

According to Matthew 13, God is removing "all things that offend and them which do iniquity." The word *offend* is *skándalon*, where we get the word *scandal* and, in this case, refers to scandalous people who create offenses wherever they go. *Skándalon* can also be compared to the native rock rising up through the earth, which trips up the traveler, causing him to stumble over a rock of offense (*Strong's Concordance*). Perhaps this is the meaning behind the stone of Psalm 91:12:

> With their hands [the angels] will lift you up so you will not trip over a stone. (Brackets added)

God, in these end-times, will protect us by lifting us up and out, away from those (the stones) who are setting snares of offense for our feet.

Although Jesus was accused of being a "rock of offense," He is the "cornerstone" for those who choose to build on Him:

> A stone of stumbling, and a rock of offense. They
> stumble because they disobey the word, as they
> were destined to do. (1 Pet. 2:8)

Another similar definition for *skándalon* (offend) in the *Strong's Concordance* is (properly) "the trigger of a trap [the mechanism closing a trap down on the unsuspecting victim] and (figuratively) "an offense, putting a negative cause-and-effect relationship into motion." Skándalon stresses the method (means) of entrapment. Therefore, these people who offend are "trappers," drawing others to the bait they have laid out for them as to ensnare them in it. The bait they use is nearly always an offense. The body of Christ should be watchful for these trappers who have bitter roots within themselves and have the potential to defile everyone around them.

Paul writes,

> See to it that no one comes short of the grace
> of God; that no root of bitterness springing up
> causes trouble, and by it many become defiled.
> (Heb. 12:15)

It is time for those who stand up in defiance against God (while gnashing their teeth at His anointed ones) to be forced to retain their own bitterness. As the great separation occurs, their rage will become only their own as they are locked outside the city gates. Jude spoke of these, saying,

> They are raging waves of the sea, foaming up
> their own shame; wandering stars for whom is

reserved the blackness of darkness forever. (Jude
1:13)

Indeed, their shame will not be shared; it will be their own. Their bitter water will not be distributed any longer because they'll be forced to hold their own toxic contents. After God removes "all things that offend and them which do iniquity," scriptures declare that it will be then that the righteous will shine forth as the sun in the kingdom of their Father (Matt. 13:43).

Trampling the Serpent's Seed

God promised in the last days that there would be healing and growth for those who revered His name, along with the authority to trample on the wicked. These promises are found in an Old Testament prophecy in Malachi:

> Surely the day is coming; it will burn like a furnace. All the arrogant and every evildoer will be stubble, and the day that is coming will set them on fire, says the Lord Almighty. Not a root or a branch will be left to them. But for you who revere my name, the sun of righteousness will rise with healing in its rays. And you will go out and frolic like well-fed calves. Then you will trample on the wicked; they will be ashes under the soles of your feet on the day when I act, says the Lord Almighty. (Mal. 4:1–3)

Verse 3 notes that the fire of God will burn the wicked to ashes. "They will become ashes under the soles of your feet when this happens," God said. The placement of the wicked under the soles of our feet signifies the authority of the righteous over the wicked and even reveals that the righteous will trample on them on that day. The word *trample* is *asas*, which means "to press, crush by treading, to tread down." The more primitive form refers to "squeezing out juice" as in a winepress where the grapes (or olives for oil) are trodden underfoot.

Lamentations 1:15 reveals that God crushes wicked (and proud) men under His feet, saying, "The Lord has trampled underfoot all my mighty men in my midst; He has called an assembly against me

To crush my young men; The Lord trampled as in a winepress The virgin daughter of Judah."

Again, the word *trampled* here refers to treading (pressing) for wine or oil, "the Lord trampled as in a winepress."

What is the relationship between trampling the grapes for wine (or the olives for oil) as it pertains to trampling on the wicked?

The manual treading of grapes is a tradition that has lasted for thousands of years and is still used in some wine regions today. It is probable that the very first winepress was the human foot, the crushing and squeezing of grape juice into a container (basin). Although there were many methods used for pressing the grapes for wine (and olives for oil), God related this crushing and extracting process to "trampling the wicked." In the same manner that a vinedresser would tread the grapes by exerting (applying) pressure to extract the juice (or oil), God does the same to all who work iniquity. This end-time act of judgment entails a crushing of the wicked that was demonstrated in a vision given to John in Revelation 14:

> After that, another angel came from the Temple in heaven, and he also had a sharp sickle. Then another angel, who had power to destroy with fire, came from the altar. He shouted to the angel with the sharp sickle, "Swing your sickle now to gather the clusters of grapes from the vines of the earth, for they are ripe for judgment." So the angel swung his sickle over the earth and loaded the grapes into the great winepress of God's wrath. The grapes were trampled in the winepress outside the city, and blood flowed from the winepress in a stream about 180 miles long and as high as a horse's bridle. (Rev. 14:17–20)

Verse 20 says that the grapes, which represent wicked people, are trampled in the winepress of God's wrath, which means they will be crushed with the feet, underfoot. Job 40:12 says, "Look on every proud person and humble him; trample the wicked where they stand."

Throughout the Bible, God has given His people many directives to bring the wicked underfoot, namely, under subjection.

When God spoke of trampling the wicked under our feet, more often than not He was referring to snakes in human form. As a matter of fact, these people are often referred to in the scriptures as the seed of the serpent. For example, on several different occasions, Jesus categorized the religious teachers and Pharisees of that day as children of the serpent kingdom: "offspring of vipers" (Matt. 23:33), "children of serpents" (Matt. 3:7), "generation of vipers" (Matt. 12:34), "brood of snakes" (Luke 3:7).

These references to "men as offspring" allude to the offspring (progeny) of serpents, men of an animal kingdom! Jesus described them as poisonous snakes who, by their words, were delivering deadly venom with the use of blasphemy. The word *children* in the examples given above, "children of serpents," comes from *gennáo*, which means "to procreate a descendant, to produce offspring, to conceive, to become the father of, to be born, begotten" (*Strong's Concordance*).

Therefore, people could be (figuratively) classified as "descendants of animals" according to the Bible. In this case, they were from "the seed of the serpent." When John the Baptist referred to the Pharisees as a "brood of vipers," he was essentially calling them a "family of snakes" or "children of the serpent" because of their venomous practice (outflow). Scriptures indicate that Cain was a child of that wicked one.

> Don't be like Cain. He was a child of the evil one and murdered his brother. And why did Cain murder his brother? Because the things Cain did were evil and the things his brother did had God's approval. (1 John 3:12)

As a result of Satan's trickery of Eve in the garden, the animal kingdom (both physical and metaphysical) came under a curse.

When God cursed the serpent, He was referring to both the actual serpent animal and to the serpent spirit (Satan):

> The LORD God said to the serpent, "Because you have done this, cursed are you above all livestock and above all beasts of the field; on your belly you shall go, and dust you shall eat all the days of your life. I will put hostility between you and the woman, and between your offspring [seed] and her offspring [seed]; he shall bruise your head, and you shall bruise his heel." (Gen. 3:14–15)

Herein marked the beginning of a new rivalry, a seed war. First, between Satan and the woman and then between Satan's offspring and the woman's offspring. Pay close attention to the words spoken by God, "I will put hostility between your offspring [seed] and her offspring [seed]." The serpent's offspring, which were Satan's human instruments, would be extremely hostile against the woman's offspring, which was Jesus, the seed that fell to the ground and died.

> But Jesus replied, "The hour has come for the Son of Man to be glorified. Truly, truly, I tell you, unless a kernel of wheat falls to the ground and dies, it remains only a seed; but if it dies, it bears much fruit." (John 12:23–24)

Because of the death of the Father's seed, which was His only Son, God's fruit harvest began to develop. God put His seed (Jesus) within the woman. Since Mary's womb was the matrix for Jesus to enter the earthly sphere, scriptures refer to Jesus as "her seed." Her seed, which was God's Word in living form, would dominate Satan's animal (serpent) offspring. God told the serpent, "He [Jesus] shall bruise your head, and you shall bruise His heel" (Gen. 3:15). In other words, God's kingdom would assume a higher vertical position over Satan's serpent (animal) kingdom.

> The LORD will make you the head and not the
> tail; you shall be above only, and not be beneath.
> (Deut. 28:13)

Jesus taught His listeners about their vertical supremacy. In Luke 10:19, He delegated power to His disciples, giving them authority over all evil, including the ability to trample on serpents:

> Behold, I give you the authority to trample on
> serpents and scorpions, and over all the power of
> the enemy, and nothing shall by any means hurt
> you.

I love this verse because Jesus provided details of our spiritual positioning: "on" and "over all." We have been made to rule over all the power of the enemy as we trample on serpents and scorpions. This includes the demon spirits and the human instruments of the serpent kingdom and scorpion kingdom.

These two contrasting kingdoms (of light and darkness) are in an incessant seed war against each other. Even now, Satan's serpent offspring (his human instruments) are still opposing God's seed (which is the Church harvest). Nevertheless, because of the cross, Jesus "crushed" the serpent's head (which symbolizes Jesus's triumph over sin and Satan) (John 12:31). The serpent striking the Messiah's heel was a picture of Jesus being wounded on the cross. Although through death Satan bruised Jesus's "heel," His resurrection bruised the serpent's "head."

Paul wrote to the Romans in his letter, saying, "And the God of peace will crush Satan under your feet shortly" (Rom. 16:20). Through Jesus, God has caused us, His offspring, to put our foot on the serpent's head and on His seed.

Subduing the Serpent Kingdom

In Genesis 1:28, God spoke, saying, "Be fruitful and multiply, and fill the earth, and subdue it." The word *subdue* in this verse means "to bring into bondage, press, oppress, tread down, squeeze, trample, tread underfoot." It's a vertical term denoting the lowering of Satan's power which operates within his human instruments. The *sub* prefix in the word *subdue* is used with the meaning "under," "below," and "beneath." Therefore, to subdue a kingdom means to bring Satan's power under God's control, whether it's manifesting through an individual under demonic influence, through multitudes of people in a common bond of iniquity, or in specific regions/territories that are covertly carrying out the enemy's hidden agenda. Any kingdom that is not positioned "under" the Most High God is of the occultic (counterfeit) kingdom of Mystery Babylon and must be brought under subjection to the Most High (subdued).

Likewise, we have been given a directive by God to subdue and rule over the serpent kingdom of this world; it is not to stand above us. "Be fruitful, multiply, fill the earth, and subdue it" (Gen. 1:28). We are to "subdue" this earth as we were originally created to do. God meant for us to oppress the enemy (the serpent) by trampling the wicked (his serpent kingdom) under the soles of our feet.

In Hebrews, Paul wrote in reference to some of the patriarchs and faith heroes of the Bible who had trampled the serpent's seed, saying, "Through faith they subdued kingdoms" (Heb. 11:33). Paul was writing of men and women who had brought satanic kingdoms under subjection to the kingdom of God. God intends for us to engage in this type of spiritual battle, even in the times in which we now live.

As the body of Christ begins to subdue Satan's earthly kingdoms that reign within certain individuals—groups of people within an institution, satanic covens, child porn rings, the drug culture, the media, and even kingdoms that control particular territories, regions, and governments—those who have been enslaved under Satan's oppressive force will gain their freedom and say as Paul said in Colossians 1:13, "For God has rescued us from the kingdom of darkness and transferred us into the Kingdom of his dear Son."

The Python Spirit (Divination)

With the ancients, the serpent was an emblem of cunning wisdom, artful subtlety, and deceptiveness, as the serpent narrated to have deceived Eve. Hence, crafty people having this seducing nature are called serpents, as they take on the same form as the spirit itself.

In Matthew 23:33, it was recorded that Jesus looked at the scribes and Pharisees and said, "You serpents, you brood of vipers!" The word *serpent* comes from *optanomai*, which refers to "an artful, malicious person who appears, becomes visible, or allows themselves to be seen." In other words, this is a reference to malicious people, instruments of Satan who "appear" in our lives with ill intentions. In Acts 16, the apostle Paul encountered someone similar; he was "met by" a girl who had a snake spirit (of divination) in her.

> It happened that as we were going to the place of prayer, a slave-girl having a spirit of divination met us, who was bringing her masters much profit by fortune-telling. (Acts 16:16)

These types of people who have snake spirits make appearances in our lives unbeknownst to us, and we must spiritually train our senses to perceive the truth. Their intentions are to choke out the living flow, the virtue that emerges from the human spirit of the born-again believer. As was the case with Paul, they meet us on our daily path to disrupt God's purposes through us. Their goal is to destroy the righteous seed (fruit, harvest).

Scriptures indicate that Paul was on his way to the place of prayer when he encountered this hindering spirit. The next verse indicates that the demon-possessed girl began to "follow him" and his accompaniment.

> This girl followed Paul and us, and cried out, saying, "These men are the servants of the Most High God, who proclaim to us the way of salvation." (Verse 17)

The truth is that not everyone who follows us is with us. Through the words she spoke, it appeared that she was supportive of Paul's ministry. Although she was saying all the right things, what Paul heard and what he discerned within his spirit were two different things. He eventually caught on to what she was, "a child of the serpent," and dealt with the demon spirit in her.

Verse 18 says, "And this did she many days. But Paul, being grieved, turned and said to the spirit, I command thee in the name of Jesus Christ to come out of her. And he came out the same hour."

The spirit within her was taxing Paul. He was grieved, distressed, and vexed. Being in the presence of this serpent spirit exhausted him until he exercised authority over it. He didn't attempt to deal with the girl but the snake spirit within her. We know for certain that it was a snake spirit because a spirit of divination was operating through her. According to *Strong's Concordance*, when you do a study on the word *divination* in Acts 16:16, it is the Greek word *puthón* where we get *python*. In other words, this slave girl was possessed by a snake spirit that influenced her to buffet Paul on his journey. Hence, the purpose of Satan's seed and those who work iniquity is to spoil God's fruit harvest (His Church).

Although these spirits who operate through human instruments are as deceitful as the serpent who beguiled Eve, Jesus has delegated to us an authority to subdue the serpentine spirits that are operating through them.

> I have given you authority to tread on serpents and scorpions and over all the power of the enemy. (Luke 10:19)

The Skeptic Who Was Trampled

There is an account in the Bible where a king's officer questioned God's power to deliver. Sadly, the aftermath of his skepticism cost him his life. The famine in Samaria was so severe from the siege that people had resorted to killing and eating their own children to survive. When the man of God, Elisha, prophesied that the siege would be over in twenty-four hours (2 Kings 7:1), the king's officer in this account interjected, saying,

> Look, even if the Lord should open the floodgates of the heavens, could this happen? (2 Kings 7:2)

This parallels the question asked by the children of Israel: "Can God furnish a table for us in the wilderness?" (Ps. 78:19) The officer's lack of faith in God's ability to deliver in the "wilderness" provoked an immediate response from Elisha. The man of God prophesied to the officer, saying, "You will see it, but you won't participate in it!"

> Just as God had spoken through the prophet, in less than 24 hours a seah of flour sold for a shekel, and two seahs of barley sold for a shekel. (2 Kings 7:15–16)

Scriptures indicate that the king's skeptical officer had been appointed to watch the gate where he was trampled to death just as the man of God had prophesied (2 Kings 7:17–18).

If only the king's officer had known that the siege would lift within twenty-four hours. However, his skeptical words revealed the contents of his disbelieving heart, causing a breach for enemy access (Prov. 15:4).

Trampled Outside the City

It will not be possible for the righteous to radiate God's glory and shine in His brilliance until the body of Christ separates from Babylon's children, the serpent's offspring. Malachi 4:1 says that it will be the fire of God that creates the separation, causing the proud and the evildoer to be lowered. "It will set them on fire." "They will be stubble." "They will be ashes." Revelation 14:18 parallels this truth, revealing that the angel who had power to destroy with fire came from the altar, giving the directive to the angel with the sharp sickle, "Swing your sickle now to gather the clusters of grapes from the vines of the earth, for they are ripe for judgment."

Notice where the wicked will be trampled in the end according to Revelation 14:20—outside the city:

> The grapes [which represents the wicked] will be trampled in the winepress outside the city, and blood flowed from the winepress in a stream about 180 miles long and as high as a horse's bridle.

The winepress of God's judgment (wrath) will be outside the city (in outer darkness) after the Church has cast her (Babylon and her followers) out. God promised Israel that He would grant her power to rise over her enemies, trampling them like mud in the streets (the area outside):

> Then my enemies will see that the LORD is on my side. They will be ashamed that they taunted me, saying, "So where is the LORD, that God of yours?" With my own eyes I will see their downfall; they will be trampled like mud in the streets. (Mic. 7:10)

The last part of this verse, "in the streets," is the word *chuts*, which means "the outside, a street that which is outside the houses of a town; from an unused root meaning to sever; properly, to separate by a wall, i.e., outside, outdoors, abroad, field, forth, highway, more, out (side, ward), street, without."

In Revelation 11, the apostle John had a vision of the wicked trampling the holy city underfoot in the last days. In order for God to judge them on that day, however, John was required to make them outsiders. He directed John, who was given a measuring rod, to exclude the outer court (by not measuring it):

> Then I was given a reed like a measuring rod. And
> the angel stood, saying, "Rise and measure the
> temple of God, the altar, and those who worship
> there. But leave out the court which is outside
> the temple, and do not measure it, for it has been
> given to the Gentiles. And they will trample the
> holy city underfoot for forty-two months. And
> I will give power to my two witnesses, and they
> will prophesy one thousand two hundred and
> sixty days, clothed in sackcloth." (Rev. 11:1–3)

"Leave out the court which is outside the temple," God said. This land will be given to the Gentiles who will trample the holy city for three and a half years. However, at that time, God will send His two prophets who will reveal to the Church their own authority to trample!

As the Church begins to turn from her wicked ways, repent, and clothe herself in white (in preparation for the wedding), the Son of Man will send out His angels to gather out of His kingdom all things that offend and those who practice lawlessness (Matt. 13:41). The wicked will be left "outside" the walls in God's winepress where they themselves will be crushed underfoot (trampled).

The fire of God's blazing furnace, through the medium of the Church, will be so red-hot and intense that it will burn up every man's work and all his idols. It will burn them like an oven on that day, and all that they have erroneously built will melt to the ground (Mal. 4). As a result of this extraction (removal), the sun of righteousness will arise and the Church will walk in a new light that brings healing and maturity. With their newfound authority, the members of Christ's body will trample the wicked, as they will become ashes under the soles of our feet. The Church will clearly understand what Christ meant when He said,

> Behold, I have given you authority to tread on ser-
> pents and scorpions, and over all the power of the
> enemy, and nothing shall hurt you. (Luke 10:19)

The Fruit That Remains

The kingdom of God has been conceptually set up on gardening principles: Christ as the vine, we as the branches, and the Father as the master gardener. Jesus revealed these truths, saying,

> I am the true vine, and my Father is the gardener. You are the branches. Remain in Me, and I will remain in you. Just as no branch can bear fruit by itself unless it remains in the vine, neither can you bear fruit unless you remain in Me. (John 15:1, 4)

Since there is only life in the branches when connected to the true vine, especially important is the image of mankind as *fruit-bearing* tree branches. The psalmist likened the man who continually meditates in the Word of God to a fruit-bearing tree:

> And he will be like a tree firmly planted [and fed] by streams of water, Which yields its fruit in its season; Its leaf does not wither; And in whatever he does, he prospers [and comes to maturity]. (Ps. 1:3)

Again, notice the words *he will be like a tree.* When a good tree develops fruit, man can pick from it and be fed. "The fruit of righteous is a tree of life," Proverbs 11:30 says. A righteous man, then, after his fruit matures, is a tree of life!

In Mark 11, Jesus cursed the fig tree because it gave an image of fruitfulness, yet it bore no fruit. It was a lie. Our lives resemble this image when we bear no fruit. Jesus spoke about these people, saying,

> On judgment day many will say to me, "Lord! Lord! We prophesied in your name and cast out demons in your name and performed many miracles in your name." And then will I profess unto them, "I never knew you: depart from me, ye that work iniquity." (Matt. 7:22–23)

Many people during that time will *claim* to have borne fruit for His kingdom, but they will be cast out, as Jesus will deem them workers of iniquity.

Jesus not only scattered seeds throughout the earth in the brevity of His ministry but He also bore fruits that proved the power and authority of God's kingdom.

> Jesus continued going around to all the towns and villages, teaching in their synagogues, preaching the good news of the kingdom, and healing every disease and every sickness. When he saw the crowds, he had compassion on them because they were confused and helpless, like sheep without a shepherd. (Matt. 9:35–36)

The fruits of Jesus's ministry were the (visible) outward signs and miracles that proved the kingdom of God was good. God has put His seed in the heart of man in order to demonstrate the same so he can become fruitful branches in the tree of life.

In the New Testament, Jesus once prayed for a blind man whose eyesight was restored to such a degree of magnification that he was allowed to see even into the spirit realm. Jesus, having made clay of His own spittle, applied it to the blind man's eyes and asked him, "What do you see?" The man replied, saying, "I see men as trees walking." What? A blind man's eyes were supernaturally restored only to see men *as trees*? Did this man lack visual perception after just having received a touch from the Lord? Certainly not. As a matter of fact, the man's eyes were so wholly restored that he wasn't merely healed but made whole. God restored not only his natural field of vision but also his spiritual. He began to see mankind as God sees them: fruit bearers. They were no longer bodies made of clay; they were fruit-producing trees endowed with gifts and callings walking around. They carried a life-producing harvest within themselves.

This is the way we should see other men. To understand this concept is to see mankind as God sees him. Human beings tend to focus on a man's brokenness, his lameness, and all that can be measured in his darkened state. However, the blind man that Jesus restored got a real glimpse of how man was created as a fruit bearer.

Jesus once taught His listeners about bearing fruit that would actually last. He spoke, saying,

> You did not choose Me, but I chose you. And I appointed you to go and bear fruit—fruit that will remain—so that whatever you ask the Father in My name, He will give you. (John 15:16)

Notice that Jesus has appointed us to bear fruit *that will remain*. Apparently, then, according to this verse, God's fruit can come up missing from our lives, just as the woman in Jesus's parable whose coin was lost (Luke 15:8–10).

The scriptures reveal that we have an enemy who is always trying to send his foxes to destroy the fruit of the righteous. "Catch the foxes for us," Song of Solomon 2:15 says, "The little foxes that are ruining the vineyards, While our vineyards are in blossom."

Here, the foxes represent those who ruin vineyards, just as Esau's inheritance was given to the jackals of the desert (Mal. 1:3–4).

In Ezekiel, God referred to Israel's prophets as foxes that spoil: "Your prophets, O Israel, are like foxes among the ruins" (Ezek. 13:4).

The primary goal for the Church in the end-time is to prepare (mature) the harvest for the gathering. However, as God's workers plant (scatter) His seeds and tend to His vineyards, Satan not only sends demonic hosts but his human foxes as well to destroy the fruit of the righteous. Jesus reinforced this truth through a parable, saying,

> But that night as the workers slept, his enemy came and planted weeds among the wheat, then slipped away. (Matt. 13:25)

Satan's goal is to destroy the seed of God's Word before it has a chance to develop fruit in our lives (and throughout the earth).

In Mark 4, Jesus used the expression *choke out the Word* to illustrate the enemy's scheme to steal the fruit or impair the growth of it.

> The cares of this world and the seductiveness of wealth and other desires enter in and choke the word and it becomes unfruitful. And they that were sown in the good ground are those who hear the word and receive and yield fruit, thirtyfold, sixtyfold and a hundred fold. (Mark 4:19–20)

The fruit that Jesus referred to, *the fruit that remains*, will only be demonstrated through the lives of those who adhere strongly to the Word of God and through those who refuse to allow Satan's foxes to spoil the vines.

In John 15, Jesus revealed that the sole purpose for fruit development in our lives is to receive the answers to our prayers.

> I appointed you to go and bear fruit that will remain so that whatever you ask the Father in My name, He will give you. (John 15:16)

Bearing fruit is synonymous with seeing the end of our faith and having our prayers manifest (openly). Until God's Word within us reaches full development, our fruits will never appear to the world. In addition, our words will fail to prove what we say, and the signs will not follow us.

The Bible refers to fruit that has reached its full maturation as perfected fruit: perfect peace (Isa. 26:3), perfect love (1 John 4:18), perfect faith (James 2:22), perfect gifts (James 1:17), perfect strength (2 Cor. 12:9), perfect patience (James 1:4).

The word *perfect* is the Greek word *téleios* (where we get telescope), defined as "perfect, complete in all its parts, full grown, of full age." *Téleios* references a maturity (consummation) that comes from going through the necessary stages to reach the end goal (i.e., developed into a consummating completion by fulfilling the necessary process [spiritual journey]). The journey involved in our personal fruit development is linked with how clearly we can spiritually see. We tend to believe the Word of God if we can see it with our spiritual eyes. The faith of God within us takes time to mature in this manner. It takes a lot of spiritual growth to reach a place where we are fully persuaded that our prayers have been answered before they manifest.

According to the *Strong's Concordance*, the clarity of vision that is reached through this process of maturation is well-illustrated with the old pirate's telescope—with all its extensions—unfolding (extending out) one stage at a time to function at full strength or capacity (of vision). So then until our faith (and other spiritual fruits) go through the developmental process and reach full maturation, we will only be able to *believe in part* because we will only be able to *see in part*. Paul taught that there was a process involved in growing the fruits in our lives. Until the fruit actually develops, we will only be able to partially see, which translates to having our prayers answered part of the time. Paul acknowledged these limitations in his letter to the Corinthians, saying,

> For we know in part, and we prophesy in part [for our knowledge is fragmentary and incomplete]. But when that which is complete and perfect comes, that which is incomplete and partial will come to an end. (1 Cor. 13:9–10)

When faith has been perfected, which is synonymous with it being mature, the daystar of revelation knowledge will arise within us like the brilliance of the sun as it reaches its height on noonday. Our faith will become strong, our patience will be perfected, and our peace will be undisturbed because we will be able to see perfectly! That which is seen only partially will dissipate in the light of God's glory because our spiritual fruit will have reached its full capacity, hence the importance of cleaving to the Word of God, lest the foxes spoil the vines (steal the fruits). Our fruits are our words (and outward signs) made manifest to the world: "So that whatever you ask the Father in My name, He will give you" (John 15:16).

Satan is always going to compete for space in God's vineyard. He always did even from the beginning in the Garden of Eden. The evil tree of the knowledge of good and evil was there right beside the tree of life. The fruit from the wicked tree was made readily available for Eve to destroy her. When mankind was banned from the garden, he was also banned from the tree that gives life.

Even now, as long as Babylon's fruit is mixed in with the fruit of the righteous, the tree of life will not be restored as was promised in Revelation 22. The Church, by allowing Babylon's branches to intertwine with the tree of life, is delaying its restoration (maturation).

John the revelator was given a vision of the tree of life that served as healing for the nations in what will be the restored Eden (Rev. 22:1–2).

> Blessed are those who wash their robes. They will be permitted to enter through the gates of the city and eat the fruit from the tree of life. Outside the city are the dogs-the sorcerers, the sexually immoral, the murderers, the idol worshippers, and all who love to live a lie. (Rev. 22:14–15)

Notice where the people of Babylon were: outside the city. It is time for the Church to exclude the workers of iniquity so that God can trample their fruits in His great winepress. In so doing, He is *destroying* their fruits!

> Then another angel, who had power to destroy
> with fire, came from the altar. He shouted to the
> angel with the sharp sickle, "Swing your sickle
> now to gather the clusters of grapes from the
> vines of the earth, for they are ripe for judgment."
> So the angel swung his sickle over the earth and
> loaded the grapes into the great winepress of
> God's wrath. The grapes were trampled in the
> winepress outside the city, and blood flowed from
> the winepress in a stream about 180 miles long
> and as high as a horse's bridle. (Rev. 14:18–20)

Especially worthy of notice is what was excreted from the wicked as a result of the extraction process. When the grapes (which represents workers of iniquity) were trampled (crushed), verse 20 notes that it was actually *blood* that flowed from the winepress, as opposed to juice flowing from the crushed grapes: "The grapes were trampled in the winepress outside the city, and blood flowed from the winepress…"

What was the significance of the blood that emanated from Babylon's fruit (which represents Satan's human instruments) after they were crushed? John saw these things in a vision and proved that Babylon the great, the mother of prostitutes and of the abominations of the earth, was intoxicated with *the blood of God's prophets and saints.* He writes,

> I saw that the woman [Mystery Babylon] was
> drunk with the blood of God's holy people, the
> blood of those who bore testimony to Jesus. (Rev.
> 17:6)

Instead of grape juice, it will be the blood of those who were murdered for the sake of the gospel that flows out. Babylon is so intoxicated with innocent blood that she will release the blood of the martyrs. She will be judged for the blood of all the innocent people she has slain. When her fruits are crushed, their blood will cry out against them for judgment.

> The blood of the world's prophets, saints, and all who had been murdered was found within her. (Rev. 18:24)

In the finality of her doom, God urges His people to celebrate His judgment against Babylon:

> Rejoice over her, you heavens! Rejoice, you people of God! Rejoice, apostles and prophets! For God has judged her with the judgment she imposed on you. (Rev. 18:20)

On that day, many voices will be raised together in heaven with shouts of praise, saying,

> Praise the Lord! To our God belongs the glorious power to save, because his judgments are honest and fair. That filthy prostitute [Babylon] ruined the earth with shameful deeds. But God has judged her and made her pay the price for murdering his servants. (Rev. 19:1–2)

God is going to avenge the blood of the innocent by trampling the grapes of the wicked outside the city. This is one of the final acts of judgment against the people who comprise wicked Babylon. As a result, the blood of those who have been martyred will be released in a stream throughout the city streets that extends for 180 miles in length and will be as high as a horse's bridle. According to Revelation 18, Babylon's fruits will be destroyed and will no longer be found by those who received wealth from her:

> And your own pleasant fruits have departed from you [Babylon], and everything luxurious and

splendid is gone from you and you will not see
them again. And the merchants of these things,
who grew rich by her, will not find them, and
they will stand opposite from fear of her punishment, weeping and lamenting… (Rev. 18:14–15)

Even still today, Satan seeks to mix in the fruits of Babylon
with the righteous fruit because he knows that noxious weeds are
highly destructive, invasive, and difficult to control, choking out
God's desirable vegetation. As the parable in Matthew 13 notes,
Satan planted weeds among the wheat, indicating that the enemy's
intention was to choke out the good plants to keep the wholesome
fruit from developing (maturing) throughout the earth.

"But for you who fear my name," God said, "the
sun of righteousness shall rise with healing in its
wings." (Mal. 4:2)

The sun of righteousness, which symbolizes the revelation
knowledge that has the power to fully restore the Church, is necessary for the development of the end-time harvest. This light will
unveil a newfound awareness (or authority) to the Church that is
likened to the noonday sun, which shines brighter and brighter as it
rises in the day.

But the path of the just [righteous] is like the
light of dawn, That shines brighter and brighter
until [it reaches its full strength and glory in] the
perfect day. (Prov. 4:18)

God made the dawning of the natural sun in our everyday morning an emblem of how the beams of light from revelation knowledge
will pierce through the obscurity of darkness. In the New Testament,
Peter refers to God's revelation as the morning star:

> We also have the prophetic word strongly confirmed, and you will do well to pay attention to it, as to a lamp shining in a dark place, until the day dawns and the morning star rises in your hearts. (2 Pet. 1:19)

Just as the "sun star" rises in the early dawn, the "day star" of God's revelatory light will arise within our hearts just before our glorious breakthrough. In addition, in the same way that natural sunlight is necessary for the growth and development of fruits and vegetation, the end-time harvest will require the sun of revelation knowledge.

The Lord promised that this day of brilliant lights, which is fast approaching, will grow the Church (maturing her fruits) as the sun from the righteous will set the wicked ablaze, leaving them neither root nor branch.

> But to you who fear My name The Sun of Righteousness shall arise With healing in His wings; And you shall go out And grow fat like stall-fed calves. And you shall trample the wicked, For they shall be ashes under the soles of your feet on the day that I do this, Says the LORD of hosts. (Mal. 4:2–3)

Notice what happens after the sun of righteousness arises with healing: God promises restoration and maturation. The Church will grow up like a stall-fed calf as she walks in a new, brilliant light from the sun! She will finally bear her fruits, the fruits from the restored tree of life in John's vision (Rev. 22). This time, the fruits will *remain on the vine* because the members of the body of Christ will have excluded the foxes.

The two witnesses will be the two (olive) trees (also called branches) that are connected to the vine at the end of the age. They will emit the oil, which provides light for the Church, in order for her fruits to mature. Zechariah 4 makes mention of these two fruitful branches. In reference to these two prophets, Zechariah asked the angel,

> "What are these two olive trees on the right and the left of the lampstand?" Again I asked him, "What are these two olive branches beside the two gold pipes that pour out golden oil?" (Zech. 4:11–12)

The two witnesses will provide light to the world, which is necessary for the maturation of the harvest. They are imperative for readying the great harvest of the end! They are the two olive trees that were seen next to the lampstand that emit oil for light in this end-time! Their words will do what they claim they'll do. Their ministries will be like that of the Messiah; they will bear fruit from the tree of life that will provide eternal life to all mankind. Their blood will be the seed for the Church. Many souls will be won for the kingdom as a result of their lives being sown (as seeds) in martyrdom. The innocent blood that will be released from their dying bodies will be added to the blood of those who were martyred before them and those who will lose their lives for the sake of the gospel afterward. Together, the blood will collectively serve as a judgment against Babylon for her crimes against the Church.

About the Author

Author Tina M. Moore has always been intrigued about the two mysterious end time prophets, also called the two witnesses in Revelation 11, who will emerge onto the global scene in due time. Their ministries will be fascinating seeing that they will perform unusual miracles and marvelous signs and wonders in the name of Jesus. Tina has always wondered how God's most anointed prophets, who pique the interest of so many, could only be mentioned in such a short passage of scripture in Revelation 11. However, in time God would reveal to her the signs that pointed toward their appearance in various places throughout the Bible. One day she inquired within herself, Is the Church prepared to meet the two witnesses or will she take part in their deaths? She never imagined that God would make use of her curiosity to write a book about His two anointed ones, urging the Church to prepare themselves for their entrance onto the world stage. Tina has been a teacher and basketball coach for over 20 years in the East Texas area, where she currently resides. She is also the author of The Doleful Creatures of Outer Darkness, which was born out of personal experience and hardship.